Advance Praise for *Then We Grew Up*

"Honest, revealing, and relatable. *Then We Grew Up* transported me back to a very distinct period in my life and will help readers reflect on their own post-college experiences."

—Brian Frons, Professor
UCLA Anderson School of
Management and Former President
of ABC Daytime Television

"A compelling read for every twenty-something. Raw, honest, and powerful storytelling hooks readers and offers a valuable outlet for reflecting on the challenging post-college period."

—Catherine Birndorf, MD,
Psychiatrist and *New York Times*
Bestselling Co-Author of *The Nine Rooms of Happiness*

"An intriguing and entertaining exploration through a pivotal and tumultuous time in every young adult's life. *Then We Grew Up* is an extraordinarily well written, interesting, and memorable story that readers will relate to their own personal journeys."

—John Gatins, Hollywood Director and Academy Award-Nominated Screenwriter of *Flight*

"Andrew Marc Berman's *Then We Grew Up* is a marvelous hybrid, a coming of age story and an advice book that beautifully captures the fugue state of one's early twenties. Join the author, a charming, talented Ivy League student, as he embarks on a touching, frustrating, comic, joyful, and bracingly honest journey from college to independence."

—Valerie Ross, Director of the University of Pennsylvania's Critical Writing Program

THEN WE GREW UP
A POST-COLLEGE JOURNEY INTO ADULTHOOD

ANDREW MARC BERMAN

A SAVIO REPUBLIC BOOK
An Imprint of Post Hill Press
ISBN: 978-1-68261-762-5
ISBN (eBook): 978-1-68261-763-2

Then We Grew Up:
A Post-College Journey into Adulthood
© 2018 by Andrew Marc Berman
All Rights Reserved

Cover Design and Illustrations by Su Jen Buchheim

posthillpress.com
New York • Nashville
Published in the United States of America

DEDICATION

*For my mentors, role models, and everybody who
has inspired me to fill the pages that follow.*

CONTENTS

PROLOGUE: THE MOVE

Black scuff marks clashing with off-white walls. Piles of dust scattered across cheap parquet flooring that had seen more than its fair share of wear. Faded subway tiles proudly showcasing all their imperfections under the harsh bathroom lighting. Discount kitchen appliances littered with the remnants of food and grease from their occasional use. Two massive holes in the living room wall that were once filled with the most critical object in the entire apartment: the wall-mounted television set.

The apartment was eerily quiet and empty. My roommates had already moved out, and I was the last one to go. We had spent three transformative years in this place, each defined by its own series of challenges and life-changing events. Twenty-two to twenty-three: the move to New

York City to start my new job and my new post-college life. Twenty-three to twenty-four: the break, subsequent second try, and final breakup with my college girlfriend. Twenty-four to twenty-five: nonstop dating, running, and distractions—anything to prevent the dreaded slow-down where I would be left alone to ruminate and reflect on the past few years.

The space had assumed a life of its own—far greater than a couple of cookie-cutter rooms and the comically flimsy doors that divided them. Those rooms were now empty, but they were simultaneously overflowing with memories from so many seemingly distant nights. Every leftover item and minute detail served as a reminder that a monumental chapter in my life was coming to a swift end on account of an expiring lease. The dim light emanating from the misshapen living room lamp was a nod to the countless evenings that I had spent watching movies with my roommates and their fleeting girlfriends. The cleared kitchen countertops were an homage to the night that one of my roommates and I fancied ourselves chefs and spent hours preparing a surprisingly good dinner. Most notably, the vacant space in my room sparked a flashback to the very first day when my then-girlfriend had helped me move into the apartment. The room, just like us, had been brimming with so many possibilities and the allure of a rapidly approaching new way of life.

I took a few minutes to reflect on how much I had grown in the confines of this small space. I was a completely different person. I was more established in my career—the prominent asset management firm where I worked had recently promoted me to the position of Associate, and I was now responsible for managing a group of nine analysts. I had more savings and financial security (which allowed me to make the imminent move into a nicer apartment). I was also more confident in my personal life—no longer at the beck and call of every girl with whom I started to develop a romantic relationship.

Although I knew that all of these things were undeniably true, I still couldn't help but feel that I was more lost, confused, and lonely than I was on the very first day that I had picked up the keys to this convertible four-bedroom apartment. Nearly three years ago to the day, I had moved into this professionally cleaned and repainted home on a beautiful summer afternoon surrounded by new roommates and a supportive girlfriend. Now I was in the exact same place—alone—and packing everything up by myself. I wondered, *where did everything go so wrong?*

That night I was scared, sad, confused, lonely, and excited all within the span of a few brief hours. I was also frustrated—incredibly frustrated. Is this what I should come to expect? Is this what happens even after you play by all the rules growing up? I thought there would be more. Much more, even though I didn't quite know what that meant.

I sealed the last two boxes shut with cheap packing tape and pushed them out into the dark living room. I climbed into bed and hoped for the peaceful retreat that only sleep could bring, but it did not come. In retrospect, I'm grateful that it didn't. As I lay awake that night, alone in my empty room with the rain pelting the improperly sealed windows, I had one incredible moment of clarity: this move was a metaphor for everything that I had experienced in my early to mid-twenties.

I was in a completely vacant apartment without furniture, frills, or finishes—I felt homeless. I was independent and had no binding obligations to anybody but myself—I felt untethered. I was stuck in-between two homes, simultaneously confronting the nostalgia associated with what had been and the nervous excitement for everything that lay ahead; I felt suspended, stuck in an amorphous and transitional state.

Everything associated with this—the frustration, the anger, the sadness, the fear—they were all necessary side effects of my transformation into becoming an adult in the real world.

This period was a rite of passage. Others had been through it before me, many were going through it with me, and future generations would have to pass through it after me. And all these people—close friends, parents, siblings, mentors, strangers—they all had one comforting thing in common: They had managed to make the move to their new home in one piece.

* * *

This night was one of the many experiences over the past couple of years that inspired me to write this book. I realized that post-college life can be amazing, but it is also hard— extremely hard. So much will happen to us during this phase in our lives, but nobody talks about it. There may be a few TV shows, *BuzzFeed* articles, Instagram posts, and Facebook News Feed stories that explore certain aspects of our twenties—transitioning college relationships into the real world, breakups, the whirlwind of dating as a single twenty-something, new cities and strange roommates, entering the workplace, managing dynamics with our parents, fiancés—but nothing speaks to the whole of it. And the whole of it can be unexpectedly daunting, demanding, and disappointing.

This book is a moment of introspection. Four years after college graduation, I still feel just as lost, confused, and optimistic as that awkwardly dressed boy who walked along with thousands of fellow peers into a period defined by ambiguity, a lack of structure, and no specific guidance on what should be done next. This is not a how-to manual for surviving the first few years after graduation, but I do hope that my experiences and the lessons I learned from them can spark a dialogue around what I and countless others have slammed up against: the shock of adulthood, the loss of clear direction, the expectation of instant gratification, and the fear that everybody but you has their entire life figured out.

The narratives that follow are my truths—experiences that have come to define this in-between period. They are divided into three distinct sections:

"Waiting on Superman" explores childhood and how the way we grow up affects the way we act as adults. Our relationships with our parents—and the superheroes who lead us—influence how we interact with others for the rest of our lives.

"The Heart" is all about connection—dating, breaks, breakups, one-night stands, friendship, and how the search for your partner can lead to the discovery of your true self.

"The Head" is work—how we navigate the professional world, manage our expectations, and embrace uncertainty.

While the stories I share are specific to my experiences, the changes they represent happen to all of us in one form or another. I hope that they can become a gateway for you to explore your own journey into adulthood, no matter how far along you feel that you may be.

PART 1:
WAITING ON SUPERMAN

ROLLING RIDGE ROAD

A screen memory is a recollection of an early childhood event that may be skewed or magnified in importance because it relates to something of deep emotional significance. To this day, I'm not 100 percent sure that the memory that I'm about to share is entirely real. But it feels so real, and I desperately want it to be. At the very least, it's a beacon from a time when I had absolutely no control. No understanding of the greater forces that were at work. I was helpless—there was nothing that I could have done, and maybe this memory is my way of making sense of the life-changing event. I want to be able to go back in time and revisit it knowing what I know now. I want to stand up as tall as I could have, look my father in his weary eyes, and tell him that everything would be all right. That we would be all right.

* * *

I was standing by the door in the master bathroom of our old house in Chicago. It was early in the afternoon, and a soft floral light flooded in through the dusty window in the far corner. The bathroom was finished with a blend of soft woods and off-white tiles, and there were oversized mirrors flanking my right and my back left. They were elevated over the cabinets and seemed to emphasize just how small I really was at the time. I was only two and a half years old, and I had no idea how big I would have to become in the next five minutes.

I had just been let into this room by a nondescript nurse (one of many in our house around this time), and I was positioned with my back facing the door. When I entered the room, an extremely familiar figure was there waiting for me. He rose above the mirrors, and the light seemed to collect around him. He appeared to be a giant of a man, towering over me with a fortitude that could never fail. He was my father.

I remember standing in that room and looking up at him for a long time. Neither of us said anything. There was a serious silence that transcended the giddiness that usually accompanied our interactions. Something was different, but

I had no idea what it could be. He stood there for a while, looking down at me from his lofty vantage point, our reflections bouncing off the mirrors surrounding us. The scene was like a photograph—we were perfectly still within a very specific frame. He took his time before he formally addressed me. Revisiting this now, I think he was deliberately trying to slow everything down. He wanted to pause—to take one final moment to enjoy what had been before he had to deliver the line that would change my life forever. Finally, after this moment had passed, he looked down, locked eyes with mine, and told me the following:

"Andrew, Mommy went on a trip, and although she loves you very much, she's not going to be able to come back."

I don't remember anything in vivid detail for a while after that moment. However, I do remember being terrified to leave my father's side for a long time. I remember begging to be allowed to sleep in his room, being unable to sleep over at friends' houses, and the anxiety that would consume me whenever he left on one of his infrequent business trips. With the passing of my mother, my father had become my only lifeline. He was my food, my water, and my air. He was my world.

My father and I were inseparable for the next ten years. We did everything together. We frequented Chicago Bulls games, ditched school for Six Flags outings, had block-wide water wars, took exciting family vacations (consisting of only the two of us), and spent countless hours playing video games together or watching PG-13 (and sometimes even R-rated) movies. I undoubtedly had the coolest father in the neighborhood, and even without a mom, I believed that I was the envy of nearly all my friends.

To me, my father was much more than "cool." He was inexplicably resourceful, wise, and reassuring. Whenever there was a problem, he had a solution. Whether it was getting in trouble with a teacher at school or getting stuck in a boring summer camp, he would fix it. And this wasn't limited only to my elementary school years. This reliability, capability, and ingenuity carried over into my adolescent years as well. The problems may have evolved from being frustrated with the disappointment of opening a new pack of Pokémon cards without a "Shiny" to my consuming fear about not getting into a top college, but he still came through nonetheless. He was a superhero to me. He never faltered, and he was always there. He truly was my Superman.

As would any kid in my situation, I became incredibly attached to him, and this attachment continued into my college years. At the ages of nineteen through twenty-two, I knew I could always text him and receive a response back within the hour. Problems with professors or disappointment with college tennis matches would disappear after talking to him. He still had the answer for everything, and he was always more than willing to step in and solve whatever it was that needed to be addressed.

Reflecting on this, I now recognize two things. One—the extent to which my father made sure that everything was "fixed" or "controlled" was his attempt at compensating for the passing of my mother. Maybe to him, if he could always be there to console, reassure, and fix everything, I would never have to experience the pain he felt becoming a widowed father of a two-and-a-half-year-old. Second—this was not necessarily in my best interest. While this was undeniably comforting, it created an overreliance on him that continued well past my preteen years. It was amazing knowing that I always had a guardian looking over my shoulder, but it prevented me from being able to develop my own footing.

On July 22, 2014, I left Los Angeles with my then-girlfriend to move to New York for my new job. My father drove me to the airport as if it were a trip back to Philadelphia for another semester at school. However, this time something was different. It was subtle, but my father had an odd demeanor about him—a noticeable departure from what I was accustomed to. I assumed it was a combination of sadness as I was officially inheriting the title of the prodigal son, and pride since I was leaving to start a coveted job in one of the biggest cities in the world (a similar path to the one he had taken nearly thirty-five years prior). Still, I couldn't shake the feeling that something felt off.

Only a few weeks later, I learned what it was. He was finally starting to let go. He had clung so tightly for nearly twenty-three years, and he was now ready to release me into the world. There would be no more lifelines on offer and no easy escapes from the realities and responsibilities that came with adulthood. While he may always be a phone call away, he wasn't going to step in and fix my problems anymore. That had officially become my job. He had given me every opportunity growing up—a fantastic education, countless lessons and clinics for sports, a loving family (which had now grown by three—I had a kind and nurturing stepmother and two terrific little brothers), great friends, and a fantastic role model to emulate. He felt it was time for me to step into a bigger pair of shoes. My father was ready for me to become an adult, but I don't think I was ready to become one.

I hadn't developed a true sense of independence or self-confidence. I may have done well in school, with sports, and with my social life, but I felt that I had done all of it with an enormous safety harness on. One that would catch me if I ever stepped slightly out of line or went off track. Abruptly, this harness was being stripped away and I was terrified.

I was left to fend for myself in New York, trying to balance adjusting to a new home, a new job, a long-distance relationship, and complete financial independence with my all-consuming anxiety about the fact that I had no idea what would come next. I vividly recall trying to resort to our old habits—I desperately craved the sense of safety and reprieve that my father had always provided. I would call him as soon as I encountered a hiccup at work or was frustrated with something that my roommates had done. He was, of course, there to answer my calls, but this time his responses were different. He offered no solutions, no quick fixes, no easy outs—only a gentle ear.

At first, I felt abandoned, but now I've learned that my college graduation came with more than just a respectable diploma. It was symbolic for the fact that I was graduating out of the comfort and security that came with knowing exactly what would, should, and even could—thanks to my father—come next. It meant that I was now the one that needed to take complete control of the various challenges that I was starting to encounter—it was officially time for me to go off on my own and embrace the unknown.

Without generalizing too broadly, I believe that most people have been fortunate enough to experience some form of safety and shelter during their childhoods. While my situation may have been exacerbated due to the passing of my mother and the controlling personality of my father, most people can relate to the concept of a protective harness. Whether it's helicopter parents, older siblings, uncles, aunts, cousins, coaches, friends, or mentors, it's the idea that every step of the way—from elementary school projects, middle school sports, adolescent rebellions, and college dilemmas—

we have had someone looking over our shoulders and offering their guidance, advice, and even assistance. These figures represent superheroes of sorts. They were most likely far from perfect, but they no doubt provided a sense of reprieve from the hardships of the real world.

Our early twenties is the first time in our lives that we're truly untethered. The structure that we used to take for granted suddenly disappears and we're left to set our own timelines. Our friends and siblings can usually offer little more than an empathetic ear, as they are just as lost as we are. And, most notably, our parents can take a step back and release us into the real world. It's not that their job ever completely ceases, but rather that they can no longer (and should no longer) offer the same shelter that they previously did because we're now in the same arena. We become fully detached from childhood, and it becomes time to step up and face adult responsibilities. However, for many of us, it can be incredibly overwhelming.

So what can we do? Everything that we're going to cover in this book—all-consuming emotions and their fleeting nature; presence and appreciation for the moment; the care, attention, and mourning that breakups require; college relationships and their timely futility; surprisingly successful relapses; celebrations without occasion; dating and character exposés; enlightening one-night stands; accepting yourself for exactly who you are; pleasantly passionate persistence;

the finicky nature of luck; respect and backbone; the fact that most people just don't care; engagements; instant gratification; dangerous gray areas; the alluring power of inertia; perspective; gratitude—they are all stepping stones along the journey to taking control of our own lives. And isn't that what being an adult is all about? We may have limited say over exactly what happens to us, but we can decide how we want to learn from our experiences. How we want to digest them, grow from them, and use them to become the best versions of ourselves.

THE SCHOOL BUS

I had just started to ride the bus to school. My father and I had moved to Los Angeles from Chicago, and it was an easy way to start meeting new kids in the neighborhood and making new friends.

I quickly learned that there was a hierarchy on the bus. The younger and shyer kids would sit towards the front, and the older and more popular kids would sit in the very back. Every day, two of the sixth-graders would take to their thrones and pick a few of the lesser pupils to tease. This was commonplace in elementary school, but even at ten years old, I knew that these kids were crossing a line. Each day, I used to come home and tell my dad about them, but as I had not yet been the subject of their ridicule, he let it sit. A few weeks later that changed.

I left the bus in tears. I was so upset, but I didn't understand why. I was usually able to shrug off petty bullying, but this had triggered something and I wasn't able to pretend like it didn't affect me. As usual, I was greeted at the bus stop by my father (he was always early), and he could instantly tell that something was wrong. He asked, so I told him what had happened.

I had been teased about not having a mom. My dad was absolutely furious. And understandably so. The line between petty bullying and cruelty had been crossed, and he had to do something about it. It was after regular hours, but he still picked up the phone and called the school, insisting to be connected directly to the principal. An hour later and he received a call back from her—he told her exactly what had happened.

The bus arrived the next day for morning pick-up. I cautiously approached it and immediately took the very front seat with the kindergarteners. I was afraid to confront the two older kids, so I gladly accepted the lowly seat. I didn't talk to anybody for the entire ride. Fifteen minutes later, we arrived at the school and I prepared to exit the bus like any other day. The doors opened and nobody moved. The principal stepped on, and she was gravely serious.

In front of an audience of more than twenty kids, varying in ages and in popularity, she proceeded to chastise the two sixth-graders that had made fun of me sixteen hours before. She told them that they would be sitting in the very front of the bus for the rest of the school year, and that if they ever made another comment to a kid that was determined to be teasing, they would be expelled. There would be no second chance, detention, or suspension—expulsion. Deafening silence. She left the bus, and we slowly filed out and resumed our day. I received handwritten apology notes from the two kids by the end of the week.

An overcorrection. She had gone way too far. Their actions were inexcusable, but they were twelve years old. They didn't mean what they had said, and they probably didn't understand its impact.

Just like the principal, my dad overcompensated for my loss. The attention, the controlling personality, the overprotective nature—he wanted to do everything in his power to try and undo the devastating reality that we were both facing. But there was no way to undo it. There was no way to shelter and protect me from the harsh truth that I was growing up without a mom.

I had suppressed this story for a very long time. In fact, I didn't even remember it until my father reminded me about it recently. I now believe it's the perfect anecdote for my entire childhood. Whenever something would hint at the cruel truth of our situation, he would curtail it. He would overcorrect and overcompensate by whatever means possible. And now, with the benefit of perspective, I'm not sure that this was best. I am forever indebted to him for the superhero that he became, but I needed to face my reality. I needed to accept it, to stand up to it, and to conquer it. I needed to know that I could.

THE RICH KID

I grew up affluently. I spent the first nine years of my life in a quiet suburb in Chicago, shielded from any sense that I had a father who was on a very lucrative trajectory. Once I turned five, he was able to partially retire and spend the majority of his time with me—I assumed that this was the norm. I took other things for granted as well: we had second row season tickets (free-throw line) to the Chicago Bulls during the Michael Jordan era, our frequent trips were usually to some sort of exotic or foreign locale, and I would always be the first to have the latest video game console or new gadget.

Our "status" didn't really become apparent to me until I was uprooted to Los Angeles at the age of nine and a half. In a city partially defined by the car you drive and the house you live in, I quickly came to understand that my father's success was a unique differentiator for me. My pursuit of tennis (a turbulent path to say the least) was overseen by a full-time coach who spent multiple days per week at our private court. Friends who would come over were immediately impressed by the size of our TVs and the seemingly endless selection of video games that were on display. Our house became the go-to hangout spot, and everybody eagerly awaited my birthday parties.

After a few years, this status became a part of my identity. It made me feel special. My father's success had brought with it a unique byproduct—an outlet that allowed me to stand out from the crowd. The main factors underlying self-confidence for most people at this age—their popularity at school, their physical appearance, their grades, their performance in sports—were also complemented by a source that I had not earned—the fact that I was from a well-off family. As much as I hate to admit it, this became an integral part of how I measured myself.

As my dad tried to soften the blow of the hole in our family, everything was fair game. His financial success gave him the rare opportunity to give me everything that I wanted. These gifts, these things, these experiences—they helped to compensate. If I asked for something, I was given it. I reveled in having my own personal "genie in a bottle." It made me feel special—powerful even. I could procure anything I wanted with a simple request; nothing was out of reach.

The excitement and joy that came from having something that others didn't have, or couldn't have, was very short-lived. As I entered middle school, my stepmom officially joined our family and started to enact her more grounded value system. At this point, it became much harder for me to differentiate myself from the other kids in my grade. My access to elaborate gifts and special outings was immediately curtailed—if I wanted something, it was made abundantly clear that I would have to work for it and pay for it myself. I was slowly forced to give up the identity that I had previously worn so proudly.

This was an extremely difficult adjustment at first. I felt that not only had my family (which until that point had just been the two of us) been invaded by a foreigner, but she was immediately targeting a vital artery that was so delicately connected to an integral part of my identity. I became confused, injured, and even resentful. To the outside world, I may have just looked like another overly privileged kid who was finally being force-fed a value system and taught a work ethic. However, to me, I was losing two critical parts of myself—the special connection that my dad and I had, and the primary method of compensating for the substantial loss that I had suffered. They were both under direct attack, and there was nothing that I could do about it.

Eighth grade was an extraordinarily challenging year, but it forced me to grow. Through gritted teeth, I began to accept that I would need to form a new identity. I chose one that was dictated by my studies and my sport, tennis. This drew me to a better group of friends, and it set me on a productive track for the rest of high school. I still may not entirely forgive the indelicate manner in which this necessary level-set was handled, but it undoubtedly stemmed from a good place and it helped me to discover (and even appreciate) a much better value system.

Today I find myself humbled by one of the most important messages that I've learned from my own personal reflection on this distinct period in my life: Outside opinions and initial impressions can be incredibly deceiving. To any passive spectator (and there were many), the adjustment that took place would have appeared to be nothing more than a spoiled kid flailing in disappointment that he could no longer have whatever he wanted. However, to me, it was so much more than that. All of the arguments, the frustration, and the sadness that came about through this transformation were an outcry against the loss of a safety blanket. A forced removal of a bandage that was covering a deep wound.

Whenever I see somebody today acting in a manner that I might not agree with or respect, I try to empathize with them. I consciously acknowledge that everybody has their own story—their own narratives and their own truths. All of their actions, their words, their intentions, their behavior—they stem from something that I may never be able to fully understand. I haven't been able to walk in their shoes—I haven't seen or experienced the things that they have.

I also try to be cognizant of false identities. The "Rich Kid" persona, something I had previously cloaked myself in, was nothing more than a weak attempt to mask something that I was desperately afraid to confront. As the layer was involuntarily removed (though I'm still mindful and grateful for all of my advantages), it forced me to grow and discover a more authentic foundation—one directly tied to who I was and who I'd become. This person, whoever he is today, is ushered in with open arms and a welcoming embrace. He might not be exactly as I envisioned him or always what I want him to be, but he still is nonetheless. I will address, forgive, and ultimately, accept him because I have walked in his shoes.

I can't wait to see who he becomes.

THE WOMEN

O ne of the most substantial effects from the loss of my mother has been its impact on my interaction with and my attachment to the important women in my life.

Let's start with my stepmom. Objectively, she is one of the kindest, most generous, and most caring people that I've ever come across. She inherited a nearly impossible task—marrying into a family with a kid who adamantly rejected the very notion of her title—and she welcomed the opportunity to raise me as if I were her own biological child.

I was so incredibly threatened by her entrance into our family that I did everything that I could to try to keep her away. When my father would offer to take her on a vacation (an offer that she would reject because she didn't want to exclude me), I would instantly respond by asking if we could go on a trip and leave her behind (this request happened multiple times). I would stage fights with her over the smallest of chores (making my bed, clearing the table, doing the dishes, and so forth), and, to date, she is still the only person that I've truly screamed at.

Despite my best efforts and multiple attempts to scare her off, she managed to stick around, fighting back with an incredibly disarming force: acceptance and unconditional love. Through all of the ups and downs, she never turned her back on me. Still, with all she has done and the extent to which she has embraced me as her own son, I find myself struggling to express my gratitude and love for her. I've never called her "Mom," and I don't know that I ever will. To me, that title is a floodgate that I'm either unwilling or unable to open.

On a recent family trip, I tried to tell her how I felt about her. I usually pride myself on being somewhat capable with my words (even borderline verbose), but I struggled to get anything out. Finally, after several awkward seconds of desperate searching, I told her that I was loyal and appreciative of everything that she had done. This is such an understatement. In many ways, my stepmom is just as big a superhero as my father, but I still have a hard time validating her with the big title.

I'm still trying to reconcile the impact of my loss and how it colors my interactions with my stepmom. So much of it is unconscious and is still suppressed. However, one lesson that I've already learned is that it's okay that I haven't processed all of it yet. I'm still working to come to terms with the reality of my situation—I lost my mom at a devastatingly young age—and this does affect who I am today. I can only hope that my stepmother understands.

The other substantial impact from my loss is how it colors my romantic relationships with women. For too long, these women became lifelines, nurturing me and propping me up so I could function well. From the age of seventeen through twenty-four, I effectively maintained two serious relationships with only a three-month break in between. These girlfriends became my world. I would evaluate the success of a day based around their happiness with me. I magnified minor hiccups or disagreements to epic proportions, tormented by the very prospect of a girlfriend being annoyed or frustrated with me. I vividly remember, both in high school and college, that I would compulsively smother my girlfriend with attention until I felt that the relationship was solid. My insecurities grew into extreme anxiety. I was unable to function effectively when relationships didn't feel perfect. The amount of physical and emotional energy that I dedicated to preserving them was completely unhealthy, and I still look back and wonder how I managed to get through each day as well as I did.

There were times when I would get so worked up that I would make myself physically sick. I'll never forget the night when I thought that my college girlfriend and I were breaking up. We were visiting New York City to look at apartments, and at the end of a very long evening, she expressed that she didn't want to try to do long-distance. I couldn't sleep. I was nauseated. My world felt like it was crumbling around me. A wound much deeper than I was willing to acknowledge at the time was being prodded, and it triggered a fight or flight response. I felt that my very life was being threatened.

This activation happened several times throughout my two serious relationships. Anytime I felt that the connection was at risk, it became so painful that it was borderline intolerable. It got so bad that I finally came up with a solution: invulnerability. How would I accomplish this? By growing into a person who was strong enough, desirable enough, and successful enough so nobody could ever leave him. In my mind, if I could make myself into a superhero, I would never have to face another loss. How would anybody be able to rationally justify leaving me if I were perfect?

So much of what I've done is connected to my young loss. Was it my fault? I still feel a sense of guilt and responsibility for something that I couldn't possibly have controlled or influenced. But how do I make sure that I'm not left again?

I can't. I clearly haven't reconciled everything yet, but I've slowly started to accept that vulnerability is a fact and a

strength. Coming to terms with this and allowing it to resonate has already inspired a growth and an appreciation for a
new type of superpower—the ability to fearlessly open myself
up with the hope of finding true connection.

THE RED BALLOON

When I was six years old, my father and I went to
one of my favorite restaurants in Chicago. It was
a gimmicky spot that had a retro theme—waiters
would wear skates and deliver comically oversized milkshakes
directly to your table. After yet another indulgent meal (we
frequented the place), I was given one of my favorite souve-
nirs at the time—a balloon.

Balloons had always fascinated me—they would try desperately to escape to the world above, but you had full control over them. You decided their fate by way of a small piece
of nylon held precariously between your small fingers or tied
to your fragile wrists. If you managed to hold onto them
for long enough, they would eventually abandon their escape

attempts and float complacently within the confines of your room. They were so simple—they were perfect.

As my father and I emerged from this restaurant oasis, I did something that was very atypical and uncharacteristic—I let go of the balloon. I stared as it ascended into the sky above us until it became a small speck of red clashing with the brilliant blue setting. At that very moment, after enjoying the freedom and seemingly limitless opportunities of its ascent, I paused, turned to my dad, pointed to the balloon, and told him to go get it. Absurd, I know. But I truly believed that he could reach it. He was powerful, unstoppable, and never-failing. Plus, flight was supposed to be only one of his countless abilities.

Nineteen years later, with so many experiences under my belt, I began the journey of writing this book, and I think that I now finally understand why this memory stands out to me as more than just a funny story from the past. At twenty-six, I may still be just as scared, cautious, and impressionable as that young boy looking up to the sky, but I am now the one chasing after that vibrant yet distant speck. I am still gathering my footing and paying my dues as an apprentice, but I'm earning my own powers. I will continue to take my heart and my head, all that they bring and all that they've already taught me, and I'll try my best to become my own Superman.

PART 2: THE HEART

THIS TOO SHALL PASS

"I want to take a break."

Deafening silence on both ends of the phone.

I felt my stomach churn—I never thought that six words could physically affect me with such ferocious magnitude. Two and a half years, hundreds of dates, thousands of hours, and the fantasy of planning the rest of our lives together came to a grinding halt during a phone call.

I'll never forget that night. It was one of the loneliest that I'd experienced in my short twenty-four years. I was devastated despite knowing that the relationship wasn't healthy for either of us. My girlfriend and I were trying to transition our college relationship into the real world while simultaneously confronting the fact that it was the first time that we were living more than four blocks away from each other (she was in Los Angeles and I was in New York for my new job). This bicoastal, long-distance relationship clearly wasn't working, but not because I didn't want it to.

I desperately did. I was hanging on to the fantasy of being able to move back to our hometown and then rekindling some of the magic from our carefree days together in college. Ones that were cultivated in a bubble with no real responsibilities—allowed to thrive without the stresses of a first job and a completely new way of life. We were locked into the same place for four years. It was a time to explore independence and sexuality, to have fun, and to learn about ourselves. Those times were still ingrained in my memory—the effervescent beauty of a newly forming romance and its seemingly limitless possibilities.

I was so sure that we would be able to balance all of our newfound responsibilities and transition the relationship into the post-college world that the six words took me by total surprise. I'm not sure if it was delusion or simply a blissful innocence, but I really didn't know that we were so close to a breaking point. Growth is inevitable after college, but I thought that we would be able to do it in tandem. We faced two distinct choices: we could grow together, flexing and bending with all of the change, or we could break. She chose break.

As those six words sunk in and the initial shock subsided, my injury and anger gave way to a new emotion—fear. I was terrified. This had been my biggest worry even as we were graduating. I had even contemplated proposing to cement our relationship and ensure I had someone by my side. But I knew that wasn't rational. Now, six months later, and all of my insecurities became reality. I had barely found my footing at my job, and I was still adapting to a new city. Was I supposed to do all of this on my own now? I had spent so much time nurturing and protecting this college romance that I had let my relationships with close friends and family suffer. I had sacrificed numerous outings with my roommates, vacations with my family, and immersion in my new way of life all with the hope of preserving something that was apparently already lost.

Once we officially started the break, my worst fears were realized and it felt suffocating. I was alone—too embarrassed to reach out to my roommates and too frustrated to reach out to my parents (who would have struggled to hide their glee as they had disapproved of the relationship from the very start). I felt abandoned—left to fend for myself during one of the most vulnerable times in my life. I felt hollow. How was I supposed to go to work, study for my licensing exams, and go out with friends like nothing had happened in my personal life?

There wasn't a choice—I had to endure. I had to pick myself up every morning and power through. This wasn't college—I couldn't choose to skip a week of classes, ditch tennis practice, or procrastinate from studying for a midterm. Skipping work or neglecting my practice exams would have had substantial long-term implications, and I couldn't afford to explore what they were. I had to get on the train every morning, walk through my office doors, and pretend like I hadn't been heartbroken just a few nights before.

Looking back on this now, I can finally start to understand the unbelievably important lesson that it taught me—*this too shall pass*. All of those emotions, the tears, the desperate feeling of loneliness, the fear—they all went away. And when I finally reached the other side, I was completely fine. This phrase means a lot to me—far more than the six words—and it completely changed my post-college life. Living these words has been empowering—they've taught me that I am able to endure the present and make it through to better days ahead.

Over the past few years, these words have become a defining phrase for nearly everything that has happened to me. Today, with the benefit of hindsight, I realize that all my experiences, even if they were extremely painful at the time, have become a part of who I am. No matter how difficult or all-consuming a setback or trauma may feel in the moment, I can emerge whole and emboldened on the other side. I try to consciously remind myself of this every day, and I'm humbled by the fact that everything—the good, the bad, the amazing, the devastating—passes and becomes nothing more than a brief chapter in a much greater narrative.

HEDGED

"Let me be the first to welcome you to Los Angeles. The local time is 10:15 p.m., and the temperature is sixty-five degrees with clear skies."

Another reconciliation. Another flight. Two thousand four hundred fifty-two miles, five and a half hours, and four hundred seventy-five dollars for the roundtrip ticket. It was a Friday night, and instead of being at a bar with friends, I had just landed at the Los Angeles International Airport for a thirty-hour trip to visit my girlfriend.

I had wrapped up a grueling week at work—the kind where you never really leave the office. You may physically depart, go back to your apartment, sneak off to the gym for a quick workout, and grab six hours of sleep, but your mind is still at your desk. You're thinking about all of the unfinished work waiting for you, and the grind that will start with the relentless squawking of your alarm in the morning.

It was quarter-end at my new job (one of the busiest periods of the year), and I had the second of three licensing exams scheduled two weeks out. I was stressed, and there was no immediate reprieve in sight. It didn't help that while my friends were planning their typical weekend shenanigans—a pregame at an apartment, a few outings to local bars, late-night food runs—I was preoccupied trying to coordinate the logistics of making my Tri-State commute from Greenwich, Connecticut, to Newark International Airport at 5 p.m. on a Friday. It was going to be an early morning wake-up, a full day at work, rush hour traffic, airport security lines, a cramped seat, ready-to-eat airline food, and turbulence—all predicated on thirty hours of insurmountably high expectations.

I was frustrated. I knew that I was voluntarily doing this to myself, but I was determined to keep the relationship intact. It was going to take more than planes, trains, automobiles, a grueling work schedule, and FOMO with friends to break me. I was going to LA to spend the weekend with a girl with whom I was in love—wasn't that going to be enough to placate any concerns and frustrations that I had? I was sure that as soon as my plane landed, I would feel right at home.

The strangest thing happened once that flight touched down though. Instead of excitement and adrenaline, I was greeted by restlessness and discontent—something felt very off. I had done this trip before, and this temporary feeling was vaguely familiar, but the volume was noticeably louder this time. I immediately started replaying everything from the week at work. Did I miss a deliverable? Did one of my managers give me negative feedback? Did I forget to pay rent? I struggled to find an answer, and it wasn't until I returned to New York two days later at half-past eleven at night that I started to figure it out.

I was running from a life that was forming right in front of me. I lived in New York City. I was starting my career at a job that I was lucky to have. I had three roommates with whom I spent almost every night. I had nearly all my closest friends within a three-mile radius. Yet, despite all this, I was straddling two coasts. I was physically present on one, while my heart was clearly on the other. I wondered if it were possible to be in two places at once, and I wished more than anything that it was. It's only with the benefit of hindsight that I've come to realize that, unfortunately, it isn't.

For more than a year, I was never fully invested in my immediate surroundings. I was hedged. Half of me was starting my new life in New York, while the other half was on the opposite coast desperately clinging to what had once been. Reflecting back on this now, I think I was actually afraid to completely immerse myself in my new way of life. What if it made me change? What if it made me stop missing my girlfriend as much? Worst of all, what if I began to really enjoy it?

At that point, the hedge would have been removed. I would no longer have had an escape plan ready—a completely different life waiting for me on the other side of the country.

All of this translated into a year in which I didn't grow nearly as much as I could have. A year in which I didn't let myself assimilate into my surrounding environment. A year in which I didn't let myself develop new friendships since I viewed them as being temporary. A year in which, other than when I was traveling, I spent weekends in the office, not out of necessity but rather out of a masochistic aversion to developing a life in New York. The worst part was that this was all done out of fear. I don't think I was ready to actually start living—I was too busy clinging to the fantasies from my previous life, the supposedly perfect relationship and the amazing, burden-free times back in my hometown.

I now know for a fact that I wasn't really living—I was merely existing. I was stuck in-between two places—the safety and the security of a college dorm room with a woman whom I loved, and the adult life that I was supposedly already living.

As difficult as it has been at times, I've learned that I need to try my best to fully engage with everything that I do. Starting my career, forming new friendships, exploring foreign cities, cultivating new interests and passions—all of these require my full attention and deserve to have a participant who is all in.

   With a little conscious effort, I've gotten better at train-
ing myself to be completely present in the moment, at fully
immersing myself in my surroundings, at removing my
hedges, and at grounding myself in my new way of life. This
mentality has given me an entirely new perspective, and it
has opened me up to so many amazing experiences I would
have been unable to see from the small window at thirty
thousand feet.

THE BREAKUP

We were officially breaking up. And it wasn't simple—cutting emotional ties rarely is. After several days of heartbreaking phone calls, she begged me to fly out to say goodbye in person. At the time, this seemed daunting. The prospect of getting on another plane, flying across the country again, locking myself in a room with a girl I still loved, and running an emotional gauntlet for an entire weekend was overwhelming.

To me, the weekend would have represented a countdown. From minute one at the airport to the last farewell at her door, a clock would have been logging the hours. We would have relived our entire three-year relationship in one marathon sitting. Nervous energy and adrenaline, laughter, sadness, sex, intimacy, longing, anxiety, anger—the whole crew would have made an appearance. I couldn't revisit it again. I did not fly out.

I was afraid. How were we physically going to be able to pull the trigger at the end of the weekend? What if we couldn't, and we were right back at square one, extending the lease of a failing long-distance relationship? I'll never forget the phone call when I told her that I wasn't flying out to say goodbye in person. After she realized that I was serious, there was deafening silence on the other end of the line—it was déjà vu all over again, eerily reminiscent of our phone call nearly one year prior when she had dropped the bombshell about wanting to take a break. Just as it had to me then, the devastating reality of the situation started to sink in for her.

If I could go back in time and do things over, I would undoubtedly change how I handled this situation. It was not fair to her or to myself. It was an act of cowardice. I was too intimidated to see her again in person, too sad to give her one last hug, and too afraid to say goodbye face to face. By not flying out there, by allowing our serious relationship to end on the phone, I almost felt as if it wasn't really over. As if the technology connecting us was simply hitting a pause button—if you never officially let something go, does it ever actually leave?

But then I'm not so good at goodbyes. I've always had trouble ending relationships. Maybe it's because I'm senti-mental, or maybe it's because I never got to say goodbye to the first important woman in my life. It just happened. One day she was there, laying in a bed in our home, and the next day I was called into a room by my father and was told that she was no longer. I couldn't digest it. I couldn't understand it. And in fairness, I was too young.

Even today, it still feels like I'm unwilling or unable to confront the reality of separation, and I'd much rather be the two-and-a-half-year-old who was protected and shielded from the worst of it. In a way, the end of serious relationships can feel like a death. The death of hope—a life that could never play out the way that I thought it was supposed to.

We need to endure our breakups. We have to live through them and face them head-on. We can't shy away from the tidal wave of emotions that will undoubtedly wash over us. We need to say our final goodbye. Only then can we start the necessary mourning process. As painful as this is, it's what allows us to heal and move on.

There is no such thing as a perfect breakup. There is also not a predefined time for healing. Friends and mentors have told me that it takes half of the time of a relationship in order to recover from it—I call bullshit. Now I simply try to acknowledge that if the relationship was, in fact, serious, I'll need an undefined time to recover from it—space where I can completely separate.

My early twenties have been full of several beginnings and endings. The breakups have not been nearly as fun as the first dates, but they have been even more important for my development. After learning from my initial mistake, I've started to endure them—to sit through every painful moment, to immerse myself in every emotion, and to try to take them head-on. With distance and time, I've also come to realize that these have been incredible learning experiences—formative interactions that have taught me so much about myself and have hopefully empowered me for better relationships in the future. With each, I've also become cautiously more optimistic that I've diminished my necessary count by one. Here's hoping.

THE RELAPSE

66 Hey—I know this is out of the blue and it's been a long time, but I've been thinking about you a lot recently. I've been hesitant to reach out, but I don't want to wait anymore. I'm going to fly back to LA in the next few weeks, and if you're up for it, I really want to see you. I'm not sure what your schedule looks like but let me know if any weekend works best for you."

It took me thirty minutes to write that text. I edited it more than five times, spoke with three different friends, and I was still unsure if I could actually send it. The second I did and the vibrant blue box said it was delivered, I was excited.

It was a nervous kind of excitement. My adrenaline was pumping, my hands were noticeably damp, and my heart was racing. I had controlled myself for exactly one year—

there were no slip-ups. No drunk text messages, no lengthy emails, no posts, absolutely nothing. I had even gone so far as to explicitly avoid checking her Facebook page or Instagram account—I was determined to try and cut her out of my life, to let myself heal and to immerse myself in my job and in NYC. Why then, after more than a year, numerous dates with other girls (including three semi-serious relationships), and hours of therapy, did I finally decide to send that text? Because I had to. I felt possessed. I wanted her back.

A few hours passed until I finally received a response. It was quite a lengthy message, complete with the usual text habits that I had come to expect from her over multiple years of dating (the "hi" with multiple i's and the "yaa"). While there was a full paragraph for me to read through, three words jumped out at me immediately: "I've moved on."

My heart sank. The excitement that I had initially felt sending that message disappeared instantly. But I wasn't ready to give up yet. What if it was a bluff? A challenge? After all, I had faced so many of these inauthentic moments with her over the years. (It's something that really attracted me to her—I love having to work for something and solve it like a jigsaw puzzle.) I responded by asking if the coming weekend would work (she mentioned that despite the fact that she had moved on, she would be willing to meet up out of respect to our history together), and I immediately booked my ticket.

The following week at work was incredibly difficult for me. I was on a different coast. Every assignment or task that I had during the week was completed on autopilot. I was trying to hit a fast-forward button and skip to our looming meeting. A combination of fear, excitement, and anxiety fueled me and made everything that stood between it seem like a blur. My mind was drifting the entire week—what would I say when I first saw her? Would we greet each other with a hug, a lukewarm and contrived hello, or would there only be an awkward silence?

The week crawled by and the day finally arrived. I don't think I've ever cared so much about what I was wearing. I ran an unnecessary load of laundry and used more hair product than I should openly admit. I was like a top that wouldn't stop spinning. I was getting more anxious by the hour, and I wanted nothing more than to be at the coffee shop that I had never been to before.

I showed up a few minutes early (something that had been somewhat uncharacteristic for me throughout our relationship—I was notoriously late). I waited outside, sporting a perfectly ironed shirt, black pants, and a fragile façade that barely hid all of the emotions that were stirring vigorously inside of me.

She pulled up in her small white car—the very same one that I had picked out for her only two years earlier. When I first saw her, I froze—this had been the very moment that

I had tried so desperately to run away from for over a year. She opened the door, and a perfectly composed version of the girl that I had known so intimately got out and went to put money in the meter. Her hair was blown out, and she was wearing a pair of well-fitting jeans that complemented her figure. A leather jacket shrouded the shoulders and arms that I had come to know so well, and big glasses temporarily masked her face as if she were trying to hide her identity and prevent unwelcome visitors from interjecting into her personal life.

Neither of us said a word to each other for the first minute. I had no idea what to say. I had both dreaded and dreamed of this very moment for so long, and I had stage fright. I finally mustered up the courage to break the silence, and the first words that escaped my mouth were a forced "Do you want something to drink?" She nodded slowly. We went inside the coffee shop, picked out an overpriced bottle of Evian, and searched for a quiet table.

I sat down with her and was immediately taken aback. She looked different. I understand that people can change and that even a year can result in material differences to someone's physical appearance, but this was something else. The structure of her face somehow seemed to have morphed. I noticed things about her that I had never seen before. How was this possible? I had analyzed her face in such a variety of settings over our three years of dating, and I had never noticed any of these details. It was fascinating to me, and I took a few moments to revel in the veil that had finally been lifted.

The next hour and a half was an absolute whirlwind. I ran the gamut of emotions from tears to laughter, sadness to happiness, and dread to relief. After spending a little time digesting all that transpired during this meet-up, I can confidently declare that this was one of the most complex emotional states that I've ever experienced.

I kicked off the conversation with an apology, and I read her a few of the passages from this book. After the first sentence of explaining why I didn't fly out the year prior, my fraying wall immediately came down and tears flowed freely for the first time in several months. I choked my way through the remainder of my prepared remarks, and when I looked up, her face was completely dry. She was cold—she didn't say a word or change her facial expression. I knew at that moment that we were permanently done.

There are a few things that I took away from this meeting that I don't think I'll ever forget. She said that I was one year too late with this apology—that there was a time where she wanted nothing more than to hear the words that I had just told her, but that this time had passed and that the words were now meaningless. She said that a part of her would always love me, but that she could never be in love with me again. That while we had some amazing times together, we were too damaged to ever make new memories. She said that she saw me differently, and that she honestly didn't like me very much anymore. She said that I wasn't nearly as nice as I pretended to be. She said that she felt vindicated—that she knew that she had done everything in her power to make our relationship work. She said that she had truly moved on.

I hadn't. During our conversation, I had an epiphany. I had been running away for the past year—both physically and emotionally. I tried to do everything in my power to escape my reality—that a three-year relationship with a woman that I loved had come to an untimely end. I threw myself into work and superficial relationships. I traveled more than I ever had before, and I filled my calendar with events every weekend. I even started writing this book—I did everything that I could to distract myself so I didn't have to face what had happened.

I was able to subsist on a fantasy for the entire year. I was still hedged. In my mind, whenever I decided to purchase that cross-country plane ticket, this previous life would be at the terminal at LAX waiting for me—perfectly preserved in a capsule that was waiting to be unearthed. To me, the relationship had never actually ended because I hadn't accepted it yet.

This confrontation was more than a weak attempt to try to rekindle the past. It was a battle between the reality I had desperately tried to run from and the illusion that I had instead indulged. A naïve part of me was still hoping that the fantasy would win, but unsurprisingly, reality found a way to triumph. I had to face the fact that my inaction over a year ago really was a definitive action. I had to accept that no matter how hard I clung onto something in my mind, facts could still force me to let it go.

I am so glad that I finally bought that plane ticket, and that I truly started listening to some of my own advice. It was time to close the chapter on the college relationship, to remove the hedge, to face the breakup in order to give myself a chance at future relationships, and to start truly living instead of merely existing. I had landed in LA with hopes of rekindling the past, but instead, I had unlocked the key to the present. As painful as it was to give her one final hug goodbye and watch her drive off, I needed to do it. I couldn't let fantasy distract me from reality any longer. I had to have hope that I was strong enough to endure, and that no matter what happened, it would pass and I would be fine at the end of it.

Robert Frost, the renowned American poet, once wrote, "The best way out is always through." It may have taken me a year, but I finally went through and I found my way out. I was free.

THE ONE-NIGHT STAND

"Do you have any more condoms?"

I eagerly erupted from the pleasantly expansive queen-sized bed and briskly made my way to the dresser. There, within an overnight bag that was carelessly thrown together, was one glorious blue box with a heroic word written across it in all capital letters: TROJAN.

I clawed clumsily at the fragile packaging until condoms spilled out everywhere, neatly arranged in successions of five with perfectly perforated dividers. They were on the dresser, on the ground, in my bag—it looked like I had just robbed the family planning section of a local pharmacy. I tried my best to shield my guest from this embarrassing sight, but I realized it was to no avail. She was staring right at me, laughing incredulously.

My biological drive was instantly triggered. *Don't you dare fuck this up,* I thought to myself. Hours of small talk, watered-down drinks, awkward jokes with strangers, two failed attempts at finding a hotel room, and a forty-five-minute drive to a completely different part of Boston had all led to this moment—inside a dingy Sheraton hotel with a willing companion for the evening. I had every intention of making the most of it.

I quickly picked up my mess and found a perfectly suitable candidate for my imminent gratification. I tore the delicate packaging open, carefully affixed it to myself, and returned to the bed to reclaim my prize for the second time of the night.

This was my first one-night stand. The infamous rite of passage. From what I had heard, you hadn't really done your twenties the "right" way until you had at least one of these. It had never really appealed to me, or at least I had tried to convince myself of that. Quick, cheap, no-strings-attached sex with a stranger? It was a dramatic departure from my usual habits of over-the-top courtship and pleasantly passionate persistence.

The night had actually started off as a complete misfire. My friends and I began drinking far too early, and our buzzes started wearing off by the time we were seated at the embarrassingly mediocre Italian restaurant that we had stumbled into. The dinner itself took too long, and we found ourselves unable to enjoy one another's company after two consecutive days of nonstop drinking.

After dinner, we agreed to try to salvage the night. We made our way to a few bars nearby, but they either had a questionable scene or an obscenely long line. With our prospects dimming, we decided to bite the bullet and wait to enter a well-known bar that featured a live band. Eventually, the tide began to turn.

The first two hours at this bar were painful. Sweaty, intoxicated bodies deliberately snaked around us trying to find their companions. A horrific band attempted to make its way through a lineup of cringe-inducing covers that were reminiscent of the distant bar and bat mitzvah circuit from my childhood. There were multiple failed passes at girls, a seemingly clear signal that this was simply not our night. Giving up on the dance floor, we retired to a high-top table in the corner near the overcrowded bar, which was serving bottom-shelf liquor. Thirty minutes later, however, and the night had taken a completely different course.

She immediately stood out from the crowd. She was short—probably 5'1"—and thin in a late-adolescent way. She wore fishnet stockings, a black mini-skirt, and a loose-fitting black long-sleeved shirt. I distinctly remember that she also wore a black choker with fake gold accents. Not a great outfit by any regard, but it worked in some strange, indescribable way.

She was a few years younger than I, but I could tell even from a distance that she carried herself with a confidence that was extremely becoming—it dated her far beyond her actual age. She seemed to have complete ownership over her body. She couldn't have cared less what other people thought of her, and she clearly had no qualms about any sort of social norms (as evidenced by the fact that she approached a table of four guys by herself).

She originally hit on my friend. A much bigger and physically imposing character, he was the clear first choice for girls going off nothing more than initial physical impressions. He entertained the idea for a few minutes, but then quickly dismissed it. I immediately swallowed any initial blows to my ego and decided to strike up a conversation. Fast forward one short hour—I already felt that I knew her far beyond the contrived and awkward connection you would expect from an encounter at a dark bar playing excessively loud music.

Two in the morning. Lights on. A voracious rustle of drunken stumbling as bargoers flooded out in the harsh light. I turned to look at my company, and I was pleasantly surprised. The fluorescent lighting, more akin to what you would find at a doctor's office, revealed nothing unsettling about this stranger. She may have been standing under a spotlight, but it somehow didn't show anything that she hadn't already made visible.

I paused for a moment and wondered how I must have looked. Sweaty, slightly intoxicated, and absolutely exhausted. Insecurity kicked in, and I was sure that the light would reveal far more than my immediate intentions. However, a moment later, something came over me. Maybe it was an adverse reaction to the emboldening insecurity, but I decided to go for what I wanted. Fuck the stereotypes, the peer pressure, and the image that I was always so concerned about preserving.

"Do you want to get out of here?" An overused and shameless line, but somehow, in the magic of that horrifically bright bar, it worked. The narrative switched. I wouldn't be sharing a cab with my drunken friends, returning to the painfully corporate hotel, and retiring to one of the two full-sized beds in our small room. My night held something far more interesting and memorable in store.

I've never been so quick to call an Uber. I even canceled the first one because five minutes was far too long to wait. I had the car take us back to my original hotel, and I figured I would just get another room. Sold out. Of all nights for this shitty hotel to be completely booked up, it had to be tonight? I quickly took her up to my room, hoping that we had somehow beat my roommate back. To my dismay, I opened the door to find him sprawled out on his bed—fast asleep in a drunken slumber. What a waste. Anyway, there was no time to delay—I had to find another venue. I quickly grabbed my bag, double-checking for that magical blue box, and ran out of the room with my company.

We traveled to another local hotel but suffered the same fate. Sold out. What were the odds? Part of me wondered if this was the universe's adverse reaction to my dramatic departure from character. Regardless, I was too far in at this point—I wasn't going to give up until I had seen this all the way through. I called several additional hotels, and finally managed to find one that had an available room. It was forty-five minutes away.

Half-past three. We walked into a formal lobby plastered with marble and banners proudly showcasing that this was a four-star Sheraton in Cambridge. I can only imagine what the hotel receptionist must have thought about two drunk twenty-somethings storming into a hotel in the middle of the night eagerly asking for a room. It didn't matter, though—I only had the impending consummation on my mind. After an abnormally long check-in process, I was given a key card to the room and a pass to one of the most memorable evenings I've ever had.

* * *

I'll never forget this girl. Although the sex itself was mediocre, she had some incredible quality about her that I think I'm finally starting to understand. She took complete ownership over more than just her body—she had an unapologetic sense of self. She knew exactly who she was, and she was in complete harmony with this person. Her confidence was infatuating. She may have allowed me to spend the evening with her, but my "visitation" status was made abundantly clear. Even when we were in the middle of the act, she appeared to have perfectly mastered the balance of letting go while still retaining some semblance of control.

To this day, I joke with my friends that she was the most honest woman that I've ever met. She went into that evening with a goal and she succeeded. It wasn't just the clear signaling that she gave off through her actions—it was a transparency that she shared with herself. The impenitent glances at the bar, the natural fluidity of her movements, the abundantly liberal and adventurous spirit in the hotel room—she was so free.

I was envious. I had spent my whole life so concerned about my image. Every action was analyzed, calculated, and deliberate. One misstep and I worried that I could lose this "unknown" that I was working tirelessly towards. In that bed, in a city that I didn't even live in, I had somehow managed to attract my exact opposite. An untamed, confident, and developed free spirit.

I haven't seen her since that night, and I honestly don't think I'll ever see her again. I occasionally stalk her Instagram or Facebook and I always laugh. She posts from a different part of the world almost every time. I don't think that she has endless financial freedom, but rather an untamed thirst for exploration and a spirit that affords her the ability to follow it. She volunteered to work as a skipper for ten days sailing through Croatia; she took residence with a group of friends in Lagos for several weeks; she became a bartender in Hvar.

Every now and then, as I get frustrated with work, caught up in drama with my roommates, or lost in my day-to-day responsibilities, I think back to this girl and what I saw in her that night. I know for a fact that I'll never lead a life like hers, but I try to channel some of her spirit. Her endless freedom, vivacious transparency, and unwavering confidence—all of which were so contagious that I somehow managed to lose myself in my first (and, to-date, only) one-night stand.

FAIR GAME

Three large trucks, seven ambiguous vehicles, and one bright red sports car. Thirty-six possible spaces on the board. The object of this game was simple—move the pieces around in order to create a pathway out. Unlock the puzzle so your car could successfully move forward and escape the traffic jam.

This was one of my favorite games growing up. It required skill, patience, and careful planning to conquer all of the various challenges. I would spend hours at the tender ages of five, six, and seven relentlessly trying to beat all the levels. Some of them were incredibly easy—three moves or less and you were free. Others were near impossible, requiring an extensive amount of help and investment in order to succeed. I look back on this game with an unusual fondness—it satisfied my love for logic puzzles (something that I had clearly inherited from my father) while also providing hours of quiet solace to myself. Today, this game holds a very different significance to me—it's the perfect metaphor for my dating experience over the past few years.

Tuesday night. New York City in the spring. I had an eight o'clock reservation at one of my favorite Italian restaurants. The date tonight was with a manager at an overtly trendy restaurant in the Meatpacking District. I had met her while I was out one night with a group of friends. She was actually working when we stumbled into the restaurant around half-past midnight. She immediately stood out—tall with a beautiful figure, a striking face, and a sense of purpose that clearly differentiated her from other patrons. I approached her while she was working, and through a combination of luck and well-rehearsed words, I managed to convince her to go out with me.

The differences were glaringly apparent within fifteen minutes of our first date. She had grown up in an extremely progressive household in the opposite part of the country. She had left home at the age of eighteen to move to New York, enrolled in fashion school, and was now quickly ascending the ranks of a vicious restaurant scene that demanded regular work hours from six at night to four in the morning, Tuesdays through Saturdays. Multiple tattoos, distinguishing piercings, an edgy fashion sense, and subtle references to her favorite bars and clubs continued to pull her further away from me.

I didn't care though. She was beautiful and exotic in a strangely American kind of way, and she represented a challenge. How could I get her to like me? What specific cards would I have to play to adapt to this unique situation? How could I subtly shift my personality, character, and demeanor to fit myself into a spectrum of date-worthy guys?

I was recreating a far more elaborate version of the traffic jam game. Consciously omitting certain things, adding a few subtle references to the realities that were specific to my life (but had no bearing on her), tailoring dates around her presumed preferences, projecting a somewhat disingenuous lifestyle—all of these were fair game. I strategically moved pieces around, pushing myself to strive for date number two, which quickly became date number six.

The end result was that we dated for nearly three months. I definitely don't regret any of the times that we had (it was actually a lot of fun), but I felt like I was on show the entire time. Every step was exhaustively calculated, deliberate, and preplanned. How many times can you distort yourself before you start to lose a true sense of who you really are?

A relentless desire for acceptance and a fear of rejection continued to drive this dangerous skill set for nearly a year and a half. It was a whirlwind. One night, I'd be a sensitive, soft-spoken, and humble kid from a small Midwestern town.

The next week, I'd be a verbose, flashy, and narcissistic hedge fund associate from West Los Angeles. More than anything, it was exhausting. I started to lose my footing, caught somewhere in between a precarious combination of clashing characters that were each vying for their time in the spotlight.

It was also incredibly isolating. Even when I was in the company of these intriguing women, I was never really present. Inauthenticity precluded immersion in the moment—I felt that I had to keep masking my true self to preserve the possibility of "earning" a second date. Careful planning combined with perfect execution meant that I would never have to face rejection, but I don't think I should have ever strived for a second date with most of these women. The subsequent dinners and outings were empty victories—all for the sake of trying to prove to myself that I had potential and was desirable. I wasn't being seen for who I was because I wasn't willing to risk showing my true self. Even the sex (a very nice byproduct of having multiple dates with the same woman) was nothing more than a consolation prize. The real prize was acceptance—a sense of belonging.

It has taken an embarrassing number of bar tabs, more dinner dates than I'd care to openly admit, and several nights ending with complete disillusionment to finally realize that I was trying to solve a puzzle with no answer. It was an endless loop—a vicious cycle that would continue to derail my true sense of self. No matter how many pieces I moved around and how many different personalities I drew from, there was no successful way out. Today I try to consciously remind myself that I don't have to be on show—there is no "winning." Even if I have to face rejection because I'm not what the stranger across the table is looking for, it's not indicative of anything more than a match that was never meant to be in the first place.

SHAKE IT OFF

66 **H**ey—I'm so sorry to interrupt your dinner, but I couldn't help but notice you. I think you're beautiful, and if you're single, I would love to get your number and take you out for drinks sometime."

Awkward silence. There was a noticeable pause that wouldn't pass. I blamed it on the unexpected interruption—it was more abrupt than usual. She was in the middle of a conversation at her table, and she had just reached for a glass of some sort of clear beverage at the exact moment that I had approached. My words had a physical impact on her. She froze in place, the mysterious drink raised halfway to her mouth—the contents were still swaying from side to side with the sudden change in motion.

She was striking. Big green eyes, tanned skin that stood out even in the dim lighting, and free-flowing, dirty blonde hair. She wasn't my normal type, but she was undeniably attractive. In the moment, I felt vindicated—I had already circumnavigated the restaurant twice in order to validate my initial speculation, and I was pleasantly surprised to have it confirmed at a closer vantage point.

There was a second person at the table—another woman who appeared to be several years older. She was also shocked by my candid interjection. There was something very peculiar about this woman—she was staring directly at me, but with a skeptical eye. I had approached several women before but I'd never seen a reaction quite like this. It was as if she could read my most illicit thoughts.

My heart was racing—I still hadn't received any sort of response. The older woman was still staring, but it seemed like her review had cleared me of any malicious intent. I saw the faintest hint of a smile—it was the most relieving and soothing sight that I could have hoped for. The younger woman noticed as well, and her entire body relaxed. The creases on her face teased an imminent smile too—an undeniably positive sign. Quickly though, any hope I had began to disappear. Her lips didn't stop curling—they went far beyond the socially acceptable limitations of a grin, and I braced myself for the inevitable.

Laughter. Unadulterated, piercing, and painfully light-hearted laughter. It was deafening. Of all the times that I've mustered up the courage to approach a random stranger, I'd never experienced this. I was frozen—what was going on? Did I accidentally confront someone I knew? Was something wrong with what I was wearing? Had I slurred my words? The older woman broke out into laughter as well. It was softer, but still painful in its own unique way. I was dumbfounded. The answer that followed provided little comfort.

"I'm seventeen. Oh, and also, this is my mom." God. Dammit. Horror, embarrassment, and a genuine sense of guilt suspended time. I felt as if I had broken some sort of law.

I threw my hands up and slowly started backing away, as if I had confronted a dangerous animal in its natural habitat. An incoherent string of banter spewed uncontrollably—"I'm so sorry. I honestly thought you were much older. I'm also only twenty-one, so that makes this a little less strange, right?"

Hopeless—the entire situation was unsalvageable. All I wanted to do was turn and sprint in the opposite direction—run out of the restaurant, flag down the next cab, and retire for the rest of the evening. The only silver lining was that everything started to make sense. That mysterious clear substance in her glass had been water. The incredulous looks from the older woman had simply been a mother's protective instinct. The girl's hesitation had been because she was so young.

I apologized again and I tried to graciously extricate myself from the situation. (I still forgive myself for lying about my age though—anything to try to lessen the awkwardness.) As I turned around and started walking back to my group of friends, I knew that the women were still laughing at me. Luckily, they seemed to share the genuine humor of the encounter.

* * *

Approaching a complete stranger, imposing on them, and revealing your intentions makes you a vulnerable target. You become exposed. What if they say no? What if they become upset? What if they simply walk away and ignore you? Nevertheless, I always prefer to cut straight to the point.

I've experienced a wide array of reactions to this very frank pick-up line: "I'm sorry; I have a boyfriend." "That's very kind—thank you, but I'm actually seeing someone." "Sure—why not?" "Thank you—I would love to." There have also been a few flagrant shuns, which to this day, I still don't understand because it's incredibly difficult to ignore someone who is talking directly to you.

I've been pleasantly surprised at how effective this approach has been—I've had several relationships that have materialized from this. One happened while I was waiting in line at a local restaurant that I frequent. The woman, a lawyer, had a fascinating background and we dated for nearly three months. Another happened at a rooftop bar at the end of the summer—this particular woman was exceptionally difficult to start a conversation with, but it ended up being well worth it (we dated for two months). The third happened at a late-night food spot in the West Village. She was a manager at a local restaurant, and we ended up dating for nearly four months. (I got a lot of free food out of it too.)

So many of my friends are completely confined to their dating apps—the virtual world seems to be their only means of interacting with the opposite sex. I've never used one—it's not that I consider myself to be "too good" for them, but rather, I prefer the old-fashioned method of approaching someone directly. There's an intangible element to chemistry that can only be experienced when you interact with someone in person.

Regardless of how uncomfortable some of these encounters may be, I continue to advocate for going up to strangers and simply introducing yourself. It's a lost art—it flies in the face of the current trend of hiding behind a small screen and indiscriminately swiping in one of two directions. Personally, I will continue to unabashedly approach strangers on the street and strike up direct conversations—my only prerequisite is that they have to be (substantially) older than seventeen.

THE GRAY ZONE

She was unlike anyone I had ever met before. She had the uncanny ability to make you feel as if you were the only person in the room. Subtle body language, fixating eye contact, a soft smile—your surroundings would blur, fading away to become nothing more than a nondescript backdrop for the encounter.

I was immediately infatuated. Her energy was infectious—distractingly wonderful. I found my usual hesitations and boundaries easily overcome—they would melt within the first five minutes of her company. I was captivated, and I craved more. Whenever I wasn't with her, I wanted to find her. I became hostage to my own phone—compulsively checking for the flash of another notification.

I held her attention for a little over a month. Several dates—dinners, drinks, outings with friends—each adding a new twist to the mysterious exposition. I tried to peel back the layers, to figure out what was underneath it, but I was unsuccessful. Before I got a chance to really dig in, she pulled back—pursuing a relationship with someone else she had met at an event that I had been invited to but couldn't attend. Fate had intervened.

Frustration, dismay, and a bruised ego led to competitiveness. I immediately wanted to know everything about the triumphant suitor. Who was he? What did he do? What was he like? It became an obsession—it's a good thing that I had a few mutual friends who could relay all the details.

As soon as they did, I became confused. It didn't make sense—every way that I tried to measure myself against the competition, I came out on top. Why did she choose him? Was my personality that bad? Had I slipped up, said something wrong, or made a mistake? After far too much wasted energy, I finally accepted that I would never have a definitive answer. There are so many intangibles with true chemistry, so I had no choice but to accept reality and stop bothering my friends with pointless reflections and narcissistic monologues.

Several months passed, each bringing a few other short and intriguing flings. Then the text came. "Hey! How are you?" The power of a simple, well-timed text is incredible. I was immediately hooked again. The conversation started—the usual back and forth. It was all leading to the inevitable meet-up.

I arrived early and reserved a table for us in the back of the patio. It was a beautiful spring day—a pleasant breeze that would have normally rendered a seat outdoors inappropriate was no match for the eagerness that comes with the slightest hint of a rapidly approaching summer. I was already a few drinks in and the buzz was helping to ease my restless anticipation of her arrival.

She walked in, her figure complemented by a dress that was just as inappropriate for the season as the outdoor table. She, too, had been drinking—I recognized it immediately. She was overtly flirtatious—her usually welcoming personality exaggerated by the liberating effects of the liquor. We both ordered another drink, and we picked up right where we had left off.

The conversation was so natural—words flowed out effortlessly, nothing contrived or forced. It was a welcome reprieve from so many other awkward dates that I had recently withstood. I relaxed. My nerves subsided, and I confidently settled in for what I knew would certainly be an eventful evening.

After we finished our first round of drinks, we decided that we should go upstairs to the rooftop bar. More drinks. Looser lips, reminiscing about our brief past, and most importantly, questions about current significant others. I was single, but she wasn't. She was still seeing the same guy that she had chosen over me. I dug in—why had she picked him? I wanted nothing more than to win her over to avenge the loss I had suffered nearly six months prior. A third round of drinks, and our chemistry became palpable—the unwavering eye contact, the subtle brushes, the elevated laughter. I quickly recognized that the night was speeding uncontrollably toward a very particular outcome.

"I'm hungry." It was half-past eight and we were both far too drunk for our own good. I Googled nearby restaurants, and we settled on a famous Italian spot around the corner. It was a celebratory meal. A bottle of wine, multiple courses, dessert—it was nothing short of gluttonous, shameless, and indulgent. The night trended onward, the hours passing and our inhibitions fading with each additional drink. We closed the restaurant and got in a car. We were going to meet her sister at a nearby bar for another round of drinks—a questionable decision considering our current state, but with little opposition, I carried on.

"You're in the gray." It was a sobering observation. The commentator was probably twenty-five years older than both of us, and we had only known her for about thirty minutes. It's amazing how many barriers come crashing down over a couple of rounds of drinks. She wanted to know everything about us. Who were we? What were we doing at the bar? How long had we known each other? When did we first start dating? I had to cut her off—I felt an obligation to correct the last statement. We were just friends and I was quick to point out that she was in a serious relationship with another guy at the moment. The commentator continued to press the topic, asking why we were out together and where the "real" boyfriend was. She was calling us out on our bullshit and I was frustrated. Who was she, a complete stranger, drunk and alone at a bar, to interject herself into the personal lives of others whom she had just met?

I became very defensive at first, and I wanted to escape. I wanted to take my "friend" and go to a different bar, an area where we would be safe from the unwelcome scrutiny from a complete stranger. However, we didn't leave, and I slowly began to accept the fact that she was right. What were we doing? No lines had been explicitly crossed, but we were certainly approaching the point of no return.

A cool spring night somewhere in the West Village of New York City. Two drunk twenty-somethings stumbled out of an overly crowded bar after more than an hour and a half of awkward conversation with an observant stranger. The fresh air was stabilizing, and they both took a moment to revel in the change of scenery. The girl extended her hand and told the boy to call a car for both of them. The boy paused, completely frozen in the moment. Which path should he pursue? His desire was obvious, but he wasn't sure how he should proceed. He was faced with a precarious decision—get in a car with a girl whom he knew had a serious boyfriend and consummate the relationship in a way that he had never been able to before, or return home alone to an empty apartment.

Somehow, in that moment, he became completely sober. The boy turned to his friend and told her that they were both rushing something that wasn't meant to be rushed. That as tempting as the invitation was, the stranger in the bar had been right. He kissed her on the forehead and chased down the next cab.

*   *   *

The gray zone. It's somewhere between what is right and wrong. How did my night stack up on that scale? Was it explicitly wrong to meet up with an old fling to try and rekindle the flame? What if you didn't know that she was still seeing someone? What if you did, and proceeded anyway— partially out of competitive spite to the suitor that had beaten you and partially out of curiosity for what could have been?

That evening, my intentions were questionable from the onset. I wanted to make her jealous—I wanted to make her feel how I had felt only a few months prior. I wanted her to question her own actions, to replay everything, and to ruminate over her decision. I wanted to win—to make her feel that she had made a mistake. I wanted her to regret choosing the other guy over me, to yearn for what we had, and to turn to me for another chance. However, I didn't go into the evening knowingly intending to hurt the other guy that she was seeing. I was vindictive to an extent, but I did not ever picture myself crossing the black and white line. I came precariously close though.

I was operating in the gray. I allowed myself to extend the evening to the point of no return, with the knowledge that she was seeing someone else. The night never should have even made its way to that dimly lit bar at one in the morning, and its outcome certainly shouldn't have been dictated by judgment from a prescient stranger.

Today, I try to think about the intent behind my actions. I proactively audit myself—what is my underlying motivation? If the answer is unclear, then I might be operating in this gray area. I've already learned that this can be a very dangerous place to be both professionally and personally. I try to avoid it at the onset, and if I catch myself in the middle of something questionable, I try to extricate myself from it. I am far from perfect at this—I have made many mistakes and I know that I will continue to make them. However, through conscious recognition, I remain hopeful that my moral compass will continue to calibrate.

THE HANDS YOU'RE DEALT

t's impossible to block out. The familiar rhythm of a song, a cool breeze, a casual glance at the date, a fading scent, a distant landmark. It happens to me all the time. On the train, wandering through the streets of New York City, walking off a plane for another brief trip back home. Suddenly, I accidentally stumble upon a gateway and I'm teleported to a faraway place and a time that has long since passed. I occasionally find myself joyously lost in what was. I close my eyes and allow myself to drift into this amorphous dreamlike state. I pause, and I embrace it, ushering the memory with a warm and exploratory welcome. I long for it—a nostalgia that physically overpowers me. Other times, I become a voyeur. I relive the memory from a remote vantage point—a new perspective that colors the passing in a different hue, forever changing what was. In rare instances, I look back with a sense of relief. I relish the fact that I'm no longer there. I thrive in the empowerment that comes only with the ability to carelessly touch and leave an event that seemed to have such a momentous impact at the time.

* * *

February 14, 2017. Three guys walk into a bar and ask for a table in the back. The bar is dimly lit, the glow of multiple television sets glaring brightly with highlights of the week's top sporting events. They take their seats, order drinks, and ask for menus. An awkward silence initially transcends the muted banter from other patrons. The three individuals don't want to be there. They're physically present, but their minds are elsewhere. They're all reliving memories—lost in the significance of a date that had been associated with so many previous relationships.

This was the first Valentine's Day in six years that I had spent without a girlfriend. It was strange, and I refused to acknowledge anything momentous about it. I quickly dismissed any reference to the holiday as contrived commerciality—a blatant indicator of my sensitivity. Work was my sanctuary. I eagerly immersed myself in menial tasks and volunteered for all assignments offered to the team.

The workday came and went, and I lost my outlet. With nothing to preoccupy me, I started to admit the significance of the date. It was associated with so many integral parts of my past. The train ride home from work became a medium to a different time. Memories from my first Valentine's Day as part of a couple came flooding back to me. I had driven all over Los Angeles picking up favorite dishes from each restaurant that my high school girlfriend and I had come to obsess over in the nine months we had been dating. I thought back to the first Valentine's Day with my college girlfriend—I had walked across the entire campus struggling to carry an awkwardly shaped vase of flowers that must have weighed close to forty pounds. I became lost in these memories. All the visceral feelings associated with them felt tangible—the sense of joy, the nervous excitement, the sexual tension—I was channeling all of it, and it was brutal.

When the train finally pulled into Grand Central Station, I decided that I didn't want to be alone. I texted my two other single friends and convinced them to grab dinner with me at an inconspicuous bar. I arrived shortly thereafter only to find that they were suffering similarly. Their eyes gave it away. They were physically present, but they seemed to be in a different world—also lost in the significance that the date used to hold.

"A toast." My friends looked at me like I was off (which, of course, I was). I told them that we would almost certainly look back on this night in the years to come with nostalgia. That in the future, when we were all in serious relationships, this night would stand out as the one outlier. No commitments, no obligations—just the three of us, with complete freedom and independence. That no matter how unhappy we may have been in that very moment and no matter how badly we wished that we were somewhere else, we had to try our best to love the hands that we had been dealt.

Miraculously, the mood switched for the rest of the night—a weight had been lifted off all of us. As ridiculous and verbose as it may have sounded, the perspective was pacifying—it was a truth that we were able to digest and even appreciate. The remainder of the dinner was a lot of fun, and I'm convinced that the evening will soon become similar to those other precious memories—a snapshot from a time when I was twenty-five, single, and unencumbered in one of the greatest cities in the world.

*   *   *

Someone incredibly dear to me once shared the wisdom that we have to love the hands that we're dealt. That Valentine's Day, my friends and I decided to embrace our present—we somehow managed to color it with the perspective that it deserved and we came to appreciate the moment for what it was. We put it in context—we would always long for something, whether it was a past memory or a future milestone, and it would be impossible at times to stop ourselves from tripping a landmine that would transport us to that distant place. However, in that moment, we grounded ourselves in the hands that we had been dealt—a night that was a fleeting, distinct blip in our lives that we would almost certainly come to miss in the future. The conscious recognition was soothing, and ultimately, empowering. I continue to try to embrace it today.

DÉJÀ VU

S he laid her hand on the table in the back of the bar. It dinged the tired wooden surface with a subtle clack, contributing ever so modestly to the other imperfections and all of the stories they painted of nights that had passed. A candle's flicker exploded into a thousand brilliant reflections off the carefully elevated stone. A newly minted fiancé.

Curiosity. Excitement. Joy. Envy. Sadness. A completely different life encased within the confines of a white gold setting. What had happened? Hadn't it only been five years? Weren't we only twenty-five? Where did I veer off of the path—take a turn for a completely different course that I had never originally intended to take?

When my phone first revealed a notification from my high school girlfriend, I thought it was a mistake. It's strange to see a name that used to mean so much flash nonchalantly across your screen. She was visiting New York for a few days and wanted to meet up. It had been five years since our last contrived encounter, which had taken place at a coffee shop. Apologies and stories had been exchanged, and our new relationships were shamelessly flaunted at each other—a fragile showcase of the fact that we had each tried to move on. An hour and a half later and we had parted as friends, setting off on diverging paths laid out via different schools, different cities, and with different significant others.

Five years passed. We were back—a dimly lit bar in downtown NYC as the backdrop this time. So much and so little had changed. She looked the same, and had a familiarly lovable, sarcastic, and cynical disposition. Her family was well. Mine was too. Her friends were fine—scattered around the country but still connected. Mine were okay—starting to leave New York though. She was working for her parents. I was still at the same company that I had been at since graduation. She had a new dog and was living in a new part of Los Angeles. I had recently moved to a new apartment with two new roommates. I was single. She was engaged.

Engaged. Instagram and its daunting interconnectivity had revealed this to me within a few hours of the actual event (it's amazing how many photographers conveniently appear at the scene of a proposal and how quickly their documentation floods social media). When I first saw the photo, I was taken aback. It's unnerving to see someone with whom you had previously been so intimate promise the rest of their life to another person.

It was one thing to temporarily suspend reality while I scrolled through my newsfeed, but there was no escaping the gleaming stone perched on the left hand in front me. I wasn't sure how to feel in the moment. Joy, excitement, and intrigue clashed with selfish introspection. Insecurity, anxiety, and restlessness temporarily won. Was I floundering? Stagnant? Had I regressed? That ring brought with it a status—she had reached one of the biggest milestones in life. She was getting married, the next chapter clearly spelled out right in front of her: wedding, honeymoon, kids, and domestic life. I didn't know where I was going to be living, working, or who I would be dating in six months.

In an alternate reality, the meet-up would have played out very differently. Similar news would have been shared by both parties—two distinct courses culminating in an eerily parallel outcome. I would have been visiting New York for a few days—a home, dog, and close friends waiting for me back in Los Angeles. I would have been engaged to my college girlfriend. A known path set out ahead of me.

My narrative had changed though. It didn't feel like it had been a conscious decision—that I had knowingly diverged from the road I originally envisioned myself setting upon. It had simply happened. I had ended my college relationship. I had forced myself to stay in what still felt like a foreign city, away from my family, friends, and the comforts of familiarity.

I was unnerved, upset, and jealous, and it materialized in awkward and overly nostalgic banter. I made us recall a fluid flashback—a replay of exactly what we were several years prior but intertwined with glimpses of what could have been. The high school drama, prom, the dreaded goodbye before college, the Tri-State bus rides to resuscitate the failing relationship, the frustration, longing, and sadness with being apart, the reparative trip with my family, and the relief once we finally recovered from the painful breakup.

After nearly thirty minutes of indulgence, I managed to stabilize myself. Reality and perspective flooded back. I awoke from the trance sparked by the flash of her ring. I thought about where we both were. She was living back in her hometown and working for her parents. She had committed herself to the next guy that she had started dating. As alluring as this may have seemed in the moment, I was independent and unencumbered in New York City—endless optionality and an unwritten path laid out ahead of me. I would still reach those milestones, but in my own due time. I had the opportunity to continue to grow and explore who I was as an individual, hopefully preparing me for better relationships in the future. This stark contrast, while initially painful, actually gave way to relief.

The meet-up was also empowering. I was revisiting one of the most significant relationships that I had experienced to date, but the charge had dissipated. There were so many nights back in high school and college when my biggest fear was that she would find someone else—leave me in her past and move on with a different person. I'd stay up in my dorm room for hours, waiting for her to return from a frat party at a neighboring college in Boston, terrified that somebody would carelessly intervene and cause me to lose the most precious thing in my life. Now I was sitting across the table from her, directly confronting the reality that she had in fact moved on. That she had committed the rest of her life to another person—permanently veering off on a different course with someone other than me. News that would have been completely devastating to me only a few years prior was able to be digested, tolerated, and even appreciated. I took a very brief moment to revel in the significance of the occasion, not for her, but, selfishly, for me. I consciously acknowledged my own growth, and I was liberated.

I left the bar that night inspired. I put her in a cab and walked back to my apartment. The city seemed to be more vibrant than usual, the lights glimmering—hundreds of thousands of mysterious sparks that gave way to so many different worlds. The flash from that ring, still ingrained in my mind, was dulled—its blow softened by the acknowledgment of my own personal growth and the recognition of the potential brimming in the deserted streets that would be filled within a matter of hours.

WITHOUT OCCASION

The branches jutted out across the view—dissecting the city landscape and throwing the glimmering lights into a disjointed frenzy. There was peace in the chaos—a disorganization that arranged itself with the promise of potential. Headlights stared off into the distance, two distinct beams shooting out indiscriminately into the distance and fading only where my eyes could no longer distinguish them from the glow of the city beneath. A half-empty bottle of champagne rested against the left front tire—two crystal glasses kissed each other delicately, their audible confrontation muted by an unwavering stare.

Her dress draped elegantly off of the hood of the car—the dark purple clashing modestly against the mint blue hue of the paint. It was fluid, morphing around her delicate figure and outlining the perfection of her shape. A flawless complexion was complemented by large green eyes—a shade that stood out even in the darkness of the remote pull-off. There was mystery, fascination, and wonder encapsulated in those eyes—a completely different way of life, a brand-new city, and unconsummated potential.

She was floating far above the lights in the valley below— clearly differentiating herself from others that had come before and those that had yet to come. She belonged out there, too unique to be tied down to anything but the city from which she had arisen. Her energy was palpable—the vivacious smile, the flirtatious laugh, the subtle accent. I caught my breath—frozen in the moment, mesmerized by its fleeting beauty and humbled by the conscious acknowledgment of the feelings enveloping me.

Time was measured only by the progress through the bottle of champagne, each new pour marking the passing of the hour. I don't think I've ever been so present. I hung onto her every word, letting them settle and resonate before attempting a response. No inauthenticity, no acting, no hedge—I was all in. Conversations were interrupted frequently by an excuse to act on the chemistry—a disarming confrontation that shut out the rest of the world and transported me far away from the scenic road in the hills above Los Angeles.

Feet not planted firmly enough, I would willingly leave the ground and drift out there with her, abandoning everything else behind and beneath. Blissful, surreal, all-encompassing—it was my perfect evening.

* * *

"What's the occasion?" An accusation. My grandfather had ambushed us from the far right corner of the living room. It was Thanksgiving dinner, and my entire family was present. The night had started early—called for 5 p.m. in consideration of several sets of grandparents and young children. The alcohol started flowing freely right from the very start, and I couldn't help myself. I blamed the digression on my company—this magnificent woman who had agreed to join us for our holiday dinner.

It had become one of those increasingly rare occasions where reality surpassed expectations. I had taken an entire week off from work (a precedent that was now acceptable considering my tenure at the firm), and I had come back to Los Angeles for the holiday. I had plans with family, catch-ups with a few friends from high school, a reunion dinner, a few sporting events, and, most notably, one prearranged dinner date.

I had known the girl in passing back in college. We were both in serious relationships at the time, but even during our brief interactions, I had felt that there was chemistry between us. When I learned that she had moved to Los Angeles for business school, I had to reach out. An innocuous message quickly turned into a long texting exchange which, to my pleasant surprise, morphed into plans for an official night out.

I certainly had hopes for how the night would transpire—candid conversation would spark chemistry which could ultimately evolve into a true connection. Maybe we would see each other again over the break—a second dinner, drinks, a night out with my friends. She might even start to like me, setting up potential for future encounters. As much as I had built the week up in my mind beforehand, to my amazement, what ultimately took place was far more than I could have hoped for.

She pulled up to the house in her small blue car. Graceful, elegant, confident, uninhibited—an evolved version of the acquaintance that I had known informally in college stepped out and I took a minute to consciously acknowledge the significance of the moment. Despite four years apart, living in different cities across the world, and an incredibly diverse set of experiences, I had managed to reconnect with the beautiful woman walking toward me, and she was now mine for an entire evening.

The date flew by and I knew that I had to see her again. Plans were set for the following night, which then turned into a date for a third consecutive evening. Fast forward through my entire trip, and I had seen her six times in eight days. My expectations hadn't just failed to prepare me for the week— they had fallen remarkably and magically short.

Standing in the middle of my living room, I couldn't come up with an answer for my grandfather. What were we celebrating? It was late in the evening, and this was the third bottle of champagne that we had opened (the two of us were predominantly responsible for finishing the first two bottles). It was very atypical for our family to serve champagne at Thanksgiving dinner, but for whatever reason, it felt so right. We didn't have anything formal to celebrate—no milestone, no notable achievement, no birthday. There was no occasion.

I finally managed to mutter some sort of contrived answer and hoped the moment would pass. It did, and with the benefit of hindsight, I've learned that I didn't need an answer. It was champagne without occasion. It was complete immersion in the moment—a celebration for the sake of celebrating. It was true connection, joyous freedom, unencumbered optionality, exciting potential, magical presence—it was the perfect embodiment of how amazing life could really be. I would gladly go back and have another glass.

BELONGERS

She rested delicately on the bed. Her stillness belied the spirit within, an effervescence somehow taken to tangible form between a top sheet and a duvet. She was simply there—effortlessly present, bound to a different plane and unaware of the magic emanating from within.

Her hands met together at the crevice of her head and neck—her legs perfectly conjoined with the slightest angle of natural bend. It was a figure in seamless harmony. A graceful and unobtrusive exaggeration of beauty—it was as if she had assumed a shape that she had always been intended to take. It was peaceful—a blissful form that made restitution for something that she couldn't have begun to consciously understand.

The light poured in from the translucent shade in the far corner of the room. It barely obscured the world outside, unable to contain the restless energy that beckoned from the streets a few floors below. The setting—framed in an unexpectedly gentle and welcoming light—had been tailored for her. White pajamas were the costume of the moment—laced, an intricate design that added a hue of differentiation to something that appeared to be so nondescript in form. Her lips were like a poem with no voice. Her eyes, effortlessly closed, were just as revealing as those makeshift shades. They hid wonder, fascination, and beauty within—a life written by change, conquest, and growth.

She was a self-sustaining piece of art—no crowds, no dividers, no protective glass—as riveting and as inspiring as anything so effortless could ever be. I found myself very still, humbled by her form and the proximity that I had been granted. I realized that this moment, this snapshot, this ever-so-brief blip—it would never leave me. It had already become a part of who I was, forever ingrained into the backbone of something far greater than the shy young man looking affectionately towards the magnificent woman lying on his bed.

* * *

In my emerging adult life, I've yet to find another collection of moments where I've felt more at peace than I did with her on those three nights. We stayed up talking about

everything and nothing. Our families, different dating experiences, the firmness of the pillows (cold memory foam isn't
great), travels, friends, poor blood circulation and freezing
extremities, goals, "sandpaper" facial hair, worries, ambitions, dreams—we couldn't stop. It was wondrous—a dramatic departure from most of my post-college life which had
been defined by constant running, ruminating, planning,
and working.

I usually found myself striving toward something—I
may not have known exactly what it was, but I was tirelessly
chasing an unknown and distant milestone. For a few magical hours on those consecutive evenings, I was able to drop all
of it. To let go. To release everything. The perfectly rehearsed
mannerisms, the orchestrated behavior, the deliberate agen-
das—they disappeared. The only thing that mattered for
those precious moments was the company that lay next to
me. I had been transported to a different time and a foreign
place, sheltered and protected from everything that eagerly
awaited outside of that pleasantly expansive bed. It was joyful—an escape as intoxicating and soothing as any that I had
ever come across.

I didn't have to try be anybody. I didn't have to worry
about making a specific impression. I was simply present—
able to bear my completely unadulterated and authentic self.
I had been heard, felt, and seen for exactly who I was. I was

enveloped in an embrace that was far more pacifying than any that I'd felt in a very long time—acceptance.

The collection of so many defining experiences that have laid the foundation for who I am—the passing of my mother when I was two and a half, the single-parent upbringing from a father who was more similar to a superhero than a paternal figure, the relocation to a different city at the age of nine, the addition of two incredible brothers and an amazing new stepmother, two very serious dating experiences that each held their own uniquely devastating endings, the unearned status that I had desperately clung onto as a means of compensating for loss, the anxiety that came with the uncertainty of not knowing exactly where I'd be living, working, or who I'd be dating in the next three months—I was able to show all of it. Nothing was masked, hidden, or altered—it simply was as it was. Because it was me.

Andrew Marc Berman. Age twenty-six. Prep school education for twelve years followed by four years at a top university. Varsity tennis player. Finance job in Greenwich, Connecticut. A life in New York City. Single, unconstrained, and untethered—free to pursue anything, as long as it fell into an acceptable range on the spectrum of the appropriate path.

For the first time in too long, none of that mattered. I felt that I had a real identity. One that didn't include any of the points outlined in the preceding paragraph. An identity that was far greater than any résumé or collection of experiences could speak to. If ever so temporarily, I had found peace—a new home miraculously constructed in that bed, in an apartment that was fractured by broken friendships, in a city that I had never truly been able to accept as my own, and with a woman who a few years prior had been nothing more than an acquaintance among thousands of friendly faces and fellow students.

To my joyous surprise, that unsuspecting young man had morphed into something far greater than he was ever expecting to become on that long weekend in that unfamiliar city. He became himself.

PART 3: THE HEAD

THE WORKPLACE

T his wasn't what I signed up for. There were hundreds of rows left. I had been at it for five hours, and there were still at least three hours of work ahead of me.

It was 9 p.m. on a Thursday, and I was stuck in an office in Greenwich, CT. I was combing through an Excel spreadsheet and manually filling in the missing cells for contact information on financial advisors. This data was going to be uploaded into the firm's client-relationship-management system and disseminated to the entire sales team to help them generate business. I had been putting it off, but it was the end of the week, and I knew that I had to finish before I was asked for a status update.

It was my third week at my first job. I was anxious, intimidated, and excited. A big-name company. An impressive role. A great salary for a first-year college graduate. It was a large asset management firm—more than one hundred and fifty billion dollars of capital at the time—and I worked on a team with some of the brightest minds in the financial industry. More than half of the firm held advanced degrees. The head of my team had a PhD and was previously a professor of economics at MIT.

My expectations had been so high for my first day. My then-girlfriend helped me pick out an outfit (it was embarrassing that I even asked for help and the selection was awful—it would have looked more appropriate at a club), and I took a train that arrived an hour before the typical start time. I was sweating profusely during the entire one-and-a-half-hour commute, anxiously wondering what my new coworkers would be like. What would their impression of me be? What would be asked of me on day one? What big-time and high-visibility project would I be assigned my first month?

Hundreds of missing cells in an Excel spreadsheet. Prospecting information. Low impact, and low visibility. Necessary for the team, though, and someone had to do it.

My expectations had been wildly skewed—not in terms of the quality of the people or of the prestige of the firm, but by the work that I would be assigned. I had completely forgotten that I was the youngest person there. They needed someone for the grunt work, and I was the perfect candidate for it. I had no work experience, very little technical skill, and I was still cutting my teeth in a corporate environment.

I had a very specific role to play, and I realized that I needed to accept it. I was part of a much larger team and a much greater process. I would put in the time and join the tens of thousands of others in the industry who had paid their dues and graduated from their analyst roles—those that had made good impressions on their colleagues and earned the right to graduate onto more interesting work.

No matter what I was assigned, I had to bring a level of attention, care, and passion that would have been the same even if I had been working on finalizing a billion-dollar deal. I had to show up early, stay late, study diligently, and do extra work to prove myself.

I also needed to accept that the idea of graduating into your dream job wasn't the reality for the overwhelming majority of us. In college, so many of my friends had lofty aspirations—professional athletes, musicians, actors and actresses, entrepreneurs—great dreams, but careers don't usually start at their end destination. In fact, I've learned that there never really is an end destination. A very senior partner at the firm, for example, earned multiple degrees, started in the biotech industry, sold his company, retired, and then returned to the workplace in the finance sector.

Careers often take winding paths, and you rarely end up exactly where you thought you would be when you began.

It's only in retrospect that you look back and realize that the entire journey has in fact been your career. And it has to start somewhere, even if it's late at night, alone at your desk, facing hundreds of empty cells in a spreadsheet.

PLEASANTLY PASSIONATE
PERSISTENCE

66 **I** don't think that he's right for our team. We've seen so many strong candidates, and I'm not sure we should be forced to make a rushed decision just to accommodate his deadline."

There were twenty-two interviews in total. It was a new record for the longest and most arduous interview process that we'd ever put someone through for an analyst position at our firm. There was no particular reason why it took so long—conflicting opinions, indecisive hiring managers, and a large pipeline of incoming candidates all contributed to what I can only imagine was a brutal three weeks for this candidate.

He had a slightly weaker background than our typical hire and his prior work experience was not directly transferrable to the role that we were currently looking to fill. He was facing an uphill battle—his résumé and performance on the initial phone screen were strong enough to merit a second round of on-site interviews, but his chances of moving beyond this stage were lower than other candidates.

After the first round of interviews, some people were very strong advocates on his behalf—they found him to be extremely likable, and he had clearly done a lot of background work on our company. I agreed with others that while he was amiable and easy to engage with, we weren't in a position to make an immediate offer. This presented a large problem, though—he had received an offer from a competing firm. He was transparent, and he shared this with us from the onset, but it meant that we had to commit to making a decision by the end of the week.

Due to this arbitrary deadline, we decided to pass on him. We weren't ready to make a final decision, and we wanted to take more time to continue searching through our extensive applicant pool. I honestly thought that I'd never hear his name again.

He was hired two weeks later.

So what happened? When our HR team member called him to relay the bad news, he reiterated how much he wanted to pursue this opportunity. He insisted on reaching out to his other offer to tell them that he needed additional time before committing (a very bold move considering his lack of leverage and the importance of making a good first impression on a new employer). He somehow convinced them to agree to this, and he asked for another chance to come in and interview at our firm.

Round two. Seven new faces, two tests, and three hundred fifteen minutes of interviewing. It must have been exhausting. I joined the second meeting to discuss whether or not we would be extending an offer. The feedback was generally positive, but we still weren't sure how well he would fit into the specific role that was available. Again, after much deliberation, we reached a collective decision that despite his strengths, we needed more time and another round of on-site interviews to see if he would fit. The only question was would he be willing to subject himself to it and push his other job offer yet again.

He agreed. He came in and met with the specific team that had an immediate hiring need, and during the interviews, he demonstrated that he had put in hours of background work—he answered role-specific questions effortlessly, and he knew more about our team than some of our recent hires. He irrefutably proved that he was willing to put in whatever effort was necessary to succeed. Everybody who interviewed him that day had reached the same conclusion: We had to hire him immediately.

The third (and final) debrief was one of the quickest that I've experienced. The decision was unanimous. We were all incredibly excited and lucky to be able to extend him an offer to join our firm. After we left the meeting, I thought about what quality had persuaded us to keep bringing this candidate in despite early indecision and timing issues. It came down to one thing: pleasantly passionate persistence.

* * *

Persistence. It is an unbelievably important characteristic. Nearly every successful person that I've had the opportunity to meet has told me that persistence is one of the defining traits that has allowed them to excel in their specific field.

Persistence can be critically effective in every aspect of our lives. Both in professional and personal domains, this trait is empowering—it allows us to overcome the frustrations and setbacks that we will inevitably face. In my own life, I attribute nearly every success that I've been fortunate enough to experience to persistence. Walking onto the varsity tennis team in college (I was initially cut after the first round of try-outs, but through repeated outreach, I managed to convince the coach to give me one additional opportunity). The promotion to my management role at the asset management firm where I worked (the initial idea was met with questions, but I put together a proposal detailing the position, and it worked). The publishing contract for this book (I was rejected by several agents and publishers before I managed to find the right fit).

To this day, this candidate's story has stuck with me. Just as he demonstrated, if we can apply a gentle, genuine, and vivacious desire to everything that we do, we too can overcome the odds when they may be stacked against us. I'll continue to apply pleasantly passionate persistence to everything that I do, and I hope that its effectiveness will continue to surprise me.

INERTIA

His head was heavy and his eyes were bloodshot. His face was ripe—gleaming with the leftover heat from the long summer day. A slightly disheveled suit draped lazily over his athletic build. His overworked briefcase was set awkwardly on the couch—neither fully flat nor fully upright—its creased leather contorted to a shape it was never originally intended to take. It flexed and withheld, and one got the feeling that it could continue to do so for some time to come. A cracked iPhone was placed on the makeshift living room table—headphones snaked around the damaged case. A muted TV glowed in the background—its blurry images flashing colorfully, creating another nondescript backdrop for our nightly catch-up.

Few words were exchanged. The standard, "How was your day?" was answered with a trite, "Shitty." "Anything eventful?" "Nope." I'd press on, hopeful for any sort of description longer than six words. "Why were you there so late?" "Had to finish something."

With a few notable exceptions, this was the typical interaction between me and one of my roommates for a period of three months. It was brutal. Work was taking a physical toll on him—he was completely dejected and wasn't his usual upbeat, witty, and sarcastic self. I felt awful for him. He had been plugging away at a job for nearly two years, and it still wasn't clicking. Persistence, determination, and a commendable work ethic had allowed him to stay at a place that was never a natural fit for him. It was a respectable role—well paying, good benefits, the prestigious brand name of a reputable company. He was learning a few tangible skills, but he was concentrating in a niche field that had somewhat limited upside potential.

His original intention (as is so common with financial analysts) was to pay his dues for two years and use the line-item on his résumé as a foundation to move on to bigger and better things. We would frequently discuss his plans of transitioning into a field that he was truly passionate about. I, too, shared in his fantasy—graduating from temporary roles that consisted of monotonous tasks and occasionally unstimulating grunt work.

The two-year mark. A momentous occasion—the "handcuffs" unlocked from the entire analyst class of 2014. Promotions, increased compensation, and—most importantly—new jobs were rampant across our entire friend group. So many people started to transition laterally. They would take several weeks off for travel, return to their hometowns, take up a new hobby, and revel in their newfound free time (something that was no longer taken for granted in the post-college era).

This was my roommate's chance. As we had discussed, he had hit his targeted timeline. He had the green light—he could pivot into another field and find something that was far more in line with his genuine interests and natural skill set. However, the two-year mark came and went, and nothing happened. He appeared to be stuck—held captive by a dangerously alluring and consoling force: inertia.

* * *

The path of least resistance—a continuation of what has been. It's so easy to be lulled into complacency, to leverage momentum and drift along a set path. Momentum is self-sustaining—empowering a specific trajectory and allowing one to stay on a known course. Initial investment continues to feed on itself. A job, a relationship, a friendship—momentum can propel these forward with less work than what was required at the onset.

In many ways, inertia is so appealing. Change is uncomfortable—remaining on a set course is much easier. At my first job, the initial year was by far the hardest. I was proving myself—paying my dues and establishing my reputation at the firm. Then time passed. I started to relax a little more. I became familiar with the steps that were required for my responsibilities. I didn't feel the same neurotic obligation to arrive early and stay late—face time started to lose its weight.

While there are certainly many positive side effects from momentum, it can breed complacency. People will stay at a job that isn't right for them because it's easy. It's so much harder to pivot to a new job and repeat the trial period, paying dues and feeling overwhelmed again from day one.

From my own experiences, I've learned that calculated and deliberate risks are necessary to evolve. Complacency is the enemy of innovation—it stifles growth. One of my closest mentors, the head of business development at a large asset management firm, is always consciously aware of how easy it is to get seduced by inertia. He frequently says that when something is working, he tries to "throw mud at it." An unusual line, but it's a reminder that we need to push ourselves to test the status quo. He is a living testament to the validity of this phrase—by remaining dynamic and constantly evaluating new business lines (even when the existing ones are doing extremely well), his firm has been able to thrive, and it still continues to grow today.

I've learned there is no comfort in growth and that there is no growth in comfort. As difficult as it can be at times, I try to push myself into areas of discomfort in the hope of evolving. Whether it's something as small as taking on a new project at work that falls outside of my normal spectrum of responsibilities, or something as big as making a career change, I'm optimistic that this relentless desire to challenge myself will allow me to grow into a new person—an individual who has been emboldened, empowered, and enriched by so many deliberate attempts to fight against such a deceptively dangerous force.

INSTANT GRATIFICATION

'm sick and tired of hearing everybody complain about how our generation has no work ethic. How we're not willing to pay dues—to put our heads down and grind. While I'd like to be able to adamantly disagree with this, I've heard it from enough different people where I've had to pause and think about it. Unfortunately, I've come to see how they may have a point.

* * *

He was brilliant—one of the smartest people I've ever met. When I first reviewed his résumé in advance of our interview, I remember that I laughed out loud—it looked fake. He had a near-perfect SAT score and had graduated Summa Cum Laude (highest honors) with a dual degree from one of the top universities in the country. He had started two small companies in college and was also an avid auto enthusiast and sports fan. After our short lunch interview, I immediately voted to hire him (as did everybody else) and he joined our firm a few weeks later.

He got up to speed at work very quickly, and within a month, he was much more self-sufficient than coworkers who had been there for far longer. I helped train him, and then continued to work side-by-side with him as he learned how to navigate the firm. As we had similar roles, I was always curious to see how he handled his workload. I learned the following: complex client requests that would intimidate and sidetrack me for days wouldn't phase him at all. Answers would come to him with little strain. He was efficient. He would get his work done ahead of even the most aggressive deadlines. He could retain the information that he had learned and would rarely ask the same question twice. I'm not sure if he had a photographic memory or just an incredible analytical skill set, but he was so capable.

I was envious—I had to work so hard to learn everything, and I was consistently applying myself to try to master topics that came to him effortlessly. After only a month, I remember thinking that he was a shoo-in to eventually graduate into one of the coveted external sales roles on our team.

He was fired five months later.

How was this possible? How did this person with such impressive intellectual ability, efficient time management, and strong analytical capabilities end up getting fired only six months after he was hired?

His expectations were wildly skewed. He had joined the firm with the misconception that he could surpass his analyst title and day-to-day responsibilities within the first year and move on to positions that were reserved for people with more than ten years of work experience. He had no patience—as soon as there was repetition in his role, he became bored and his attitude suffered noticeably. He was ambitious to a fault—he saw far beyond the job that he was hired to do after only a few months of working.

A large part of me empathized with him. Having had been in a similar role for over a year and a half, I was also a little bored and frustrated. Every morning as I set off for my hour-and-a-half commute via two separate trains, I gladly entertained escapism fantasies of being able to surpass the monotonous day-to-day work that I had felt that I had already mastered. I wanted nothing more than to be able to flip a switch and skip this part of my career and the dues that I knew I was expected to pay. However, I've recently come to appreciate the importance of being able to delay gratification—to have patience, persistence, and work ethic. My coworker may have had a far higher IQ than I, but he also had his sights set on overnight success.

I've learned so much about my peers, coworkers, and friends by watching and listening to them over the past few years, and now, unfortunately, I believe the following: we have become a generation obsessed with overnight success.

I don't think that we're entirely at fault for this. With the advent of social media, it's so easy to access highlights reels of everybody else's lives. Facebook, Instagram, Snapchat, and Twitter have practically become forums where people can create collages of their most enthralling moments. No matter what we're doing, we can always log on and find someone else our age who is doing something far more exciting or interesting.

All of this translates into the workplace as well. Our generation has seen the expansion of the tech industry and the birth of Silicon Valley, an industry where young computer programmers (sometimes even younger than eighteen) are able to create apps and social networking sites and sell them to major companies for thousands, millions, or even billions of dollars.

Watching the outrageous success of others in these outlets has, in a sense, corrupted our own work ethic. Why do we work long hours, endure tiresome commutes, and grind away when it looks as if everybody else is living a better life than us? (And, in many circumstances, they don't *appear* to have put in much work for it.)

I can't begin to tell you how many friends I have who come to me fantasizing about launching their own app, becoming a star, or starting their own investment firm as a means for getting rich and retiring within a few years. One of my close friends, twenty-five, has already worked four different jobs post-college. She joins start-up companies and immediately jumps ship as soon as it appears that they won't raise enough money from investors to expand as fast as they want. She has even removed a few brief stints from her résumé so as not to hurt her chances of finding her next four-month employment scheme.

However, thinking about every truly successful person that I've met throughout my life, I can't think of one who hasn't paid his or her dues. Who didn't have failures along the way. Who didn't endure countless years of working jobs that he or she didn't necessarily love while living a less-than-desirable lifestyle. I'm sure that there are people who actually did have these lottery-winner type experiences with their careers—enjoying overnight success and living the lifestyle that we see splashed on the Instagram page of a celebrity or tech mogul. But these are the extreme minority. They are not the benchmark—they don't represent the path that we will almost certainly have to take to get to where we want to be.

In college, I took an intermediate-level behavioral psychology course. One of the studies that stood out to me the most was The Marshmallow Test. In this Stanford experiment, the scientists took a group of young children—approximately four to six years old—and placed them in observation rooms. Each experimenter then took a single marshmallow and placed it in front of the excitable child with the following instructions: "If you can wait to eat this marshmallow until I return, I'll give you two." The monitor then exited the room, and each kid was left alone staring longingly at the delicious treat.

This study is designed to test the ability of children to delay gratification. If they could demonstrate patience and resolve, they would double their payoff. If they could resist temptation in the short run, they would end up with a superior outcome in the long run. Of the tested children, approximately half of them ate the marshmallow immediately while the others were able to wait. The experimenters then tracked the progress of these kids throughout their development. Unsurprisingly, there was a direct correlation between the success of these kids—their performance in high school—and their ability to delay gratification. Those who were able to wait to eat the marshmallow outperformed those who weren't.

I believe this experiment is directly applicable to our experience in our early to mid-twenties. If we can delay gratification, resist the temptation to immediately graduate from the monotonous busy work of a first role, avoid the pitfalls of pursuing get-rich-quick schemes and patiently pay our dues, we, too, can reap the rewards of a more successful future.

As those young children and my twenty-three-year-old former coworker proved, sometimes it really is better to put our
heads down and wait to eat the marshmallow.

LUCK

n March 2017, Snap Inc. filed for their IPO (initial public offering) and launched at a valuation of approximately 19.7 billion dollars. At the opening bell of the New York Stock Exchange on Thursday, March 2, Evan Spiegel and his cofounder, Bobby Murphy, were each rewarded with over five billion dollars on paper. They were twenty-six and twenty-seven.

How did this happen? There was obviously huge talent involved, but I would argue that luck played the role of a silent third partner that had at least as great a contribution as either of the two founders.

The extremely abbreviated history of Snapchat is the following: During their time at Stanford, Spiegel, Murphy, and a friend came up with an idea for an app to make pictures disappear from cellphones. Rumors propagate that this app was originally created as a sexting tool—a venue to share naked pictures that couldn't haunt you for longer than the ten seconds that they were visible. This app originally launched under the name of "Picaboo," and it immediately generated traction. As you know, this eventually morphed into Snapchat, an app that allows users to send photos and videos that disappear after a few seconds. This app has become one of the most widely used apps in the world with more than one hundred million daily active users. Evan Spiegel and Bobby Murphy essentially won the lottery with an exponentially greater payoff.

There were hundreds of alternate realities that could have diverted their success. Spiegel or Murphy could have attended a different college, preventing the idea from ever officially developing in the first place. Or they could have come up with the same idea and they could have developed the exact same app. They could have released the app, marketed it, and still raised money in their first fundraising round. However, instead of the app spreading through the tween population like wildfire, it could have been dismissed by the popular girls at middle schools and died out. Or it could have been discovered by Facebook in its infancy stage, and they could have released a similar product that would have completely ruined Snapchat's chances of becoming a household name. A thousand different scenarios could have played out, and nine hundred ninety-nine of them would have resulted in a reality that was far less glamorous and enriching for the two founders.

The point of this story is to illustrate the power of luck—in almost every circumstance, the role of luck is ultimately as large as diligence, prudence, and intelligence.

Luck doesn't only play a role in monetary success either—it plays a role in all avenues of our lives. Consider dating. On a given Saturday night in NYC, there are hundreds of different bars to choose from. Each bar attracts a different group of people and will translate into a unique evening out.

Let's look at an example: a guy chooses to go to a particular bar in the West Village with friends on a Saturday night. Once there, he meets a recently single girl out with her friends. They end up hitting it off, and they start a long and incredible relationship. Now, let's consider all the variables that were at play: one, the specific bar choice; two, the time of the evening when both our protagonist and leading lady decide to go there; three, the coincidence that both characters happen to meet once inside this extremely loud and crowded venue; and four, the fact that both of them are single and are open to finding a new relationship.

The role of luck has always been frustrating and intimidating to me. It is alarming that no matter how hard you work at something and no matter how badly you want something, there can never be a guarantee of accomplishment. This is especially relevant as we enter the real world for the first time—the odds of everybody succeeding at their jobs, finding a rewarding romantic relationship, and realizing their dreams are by no means guaranteed. No matter how hard we work for something, there is this intangible element of luck that is required for true success.

I look at some of the role models in my life—my father, my mentor, one of my closest friends—and I consider the incredible role that luck played in allowing them to reach where they are today.

A simple tennis lesson that my father substituted for led to an introduction to his future business partners. They happened to be looking for a recent college graduate who would be able to move out to New York City on a whim and participate in a brand-new business venture. This seemingly unremarkable tennis lesson led to an introduction, a relocation, a successful ten-year endeavor in an options trading firm, a move to Chicago to start a real estate company with the same partners, and, most importantly for me at least, the introduction to my mother. I am eternally grateful that someone was willing to pay my dad for his slightly-above-average tennis talents at the time.

My mentor managed to convince three of his coworkers to leave a very lucrative and reliable job in the late 1990s to launch a new investment firm. Within the first six months of opening, they lost approximately half the assets that they were managing and nearly went out of business. A market reversal allowed the firm to recoup their losses and stay in business—the firm has now flourished for more than eighteen years. This near-death experience at inception led to an incredibly humble and diversified investment approach that helped to grow the company into one of the largest and most successful asset management firms in the world.

One of my closest friends was unhappy working at an accounting firm in New York. She happened to live across the hall from a motivated and ambitious entrepreneur who had just turned down an offer from Mark Cuban on *Shark Tank*. That television appearance led to a rapid expansion of his business, and he

needed additional employees. He ended
up hiring her to take on a senior role at
his company, and although she is no longer at that firm, this opportunity completely redirected her career path.

Luck and the uncertainty it brings can be paralyzing
during a period as delicate as our early twenties. What's the
point of completely throwing yourself into something if there
is such a wildcard in play? Why do we work long hours, invest
in ourselves, go out to crowded bars, and continue to pursue
our goals if there is no guarantee that they'll be realized?

While we can never secure an explicit outcome, there are
things that we can do to guarantee—with 100 percent certainly—that we increase our chances at succeeding. When we
invest in ourselves, put in the extra hours at work, go all-in
with a relationship, or study diligently for a graduate school
entrance test, we guarantee that we're at least substantially
increasing our chances at achieving what we want.

It has been so hard for me to relinquish control and to
accept the monumental role that luck has in my life. I may
never achieve all of my ambitions, I might fall short of others
who have come before me, and it could all end up happen-
ing because of this extremely finicky partner. All I can do is
explore my options, lay down the groundwork, and try to
stack the odds in my favor.

NOBODY CARES

A fifteen-minute acceptance speech. I timed it. Sentences blurred into one another—nondescript words strung together in a seemingly never-ending sequence of code that desperately needed to be broken. Bleak faces around the room. The person to my left was completely captivated by the college football game he was streaming on his phone. Audible whispers were erupting from the adjacent table. Young children were bouncing impatiently on their parents' laps. Restless dates were playing flirtatiously with their company. My eyes were glazing over—I couldn't bring myself to pay attention.

It was a Hall-of-Fame induction ceremony for former alumni at my alma mater's tennis program. There were approximately one hundred people seated at twelve tables that were erratically scattered across the floor of a converted basketball gymnasium. Tacky blue tarps were draped over each table and a campus-led catering company served questionable food given the one hundred fifty dollars-per-person ticket price for the event.

We had ten inductees to get through—each entitled to say a few words regarding his or her experience on the team. The event had been progressing at an appropriate pace—grateful but self-aware recipients had taken the podium to share a few words reminiscing about their years in the program. Their speeches weren't very interesting, but they were certainly tolerable. As the moderator continued to make his way through all of the honorees, a shared hope transcended the audience—we knew that we were almost at the finish line. Eight speakers had already given their remarks, leaving us with only two more. Then it was his turn.

The man was in his early sixties and he had flown from California to Pennsylvania for the event. He was running a tennis program at a small club in an affluent town, and he had dedicated his entire life to the sport that he clearly loved so much. When he was called up to the stage, he climbed the stairs as if the awkwardly vacant basketball gymnasium had morphed into the Dolby Theatre for the Oscars. In many ways, his enthusiasm was endearing. However, it couldn't offset the longwinded, meandering speech that followed.

He wouldn't stop talking. Stories ranged everywhere from his first year on the team to his personal relationship with the former coach. Spats with old teammates, current employment in the tennis industry, and his family were covered as well. The speech was self-indulgent to the point that it became narcissistic. There was no malice, but his lack of self-awareness was shocking.

Part of me sympathized with him. He had traveled so far to attend this event, and the team had evidently left a substantial mark on his life. This may have been one of his most prized moments. I was rooting for him. I wanted the audience, myself included, to become fully invested in his stories—to start pulling for him. Engaged and enthusiastic listeners could have made this man's year. This was his fifteen minutes—his moment in the spotlight. I wasn't sure how many others he had experienced, and I desperately wanted everybody to play along.

We each held a unique power for this man—we had the rare opportunity to give a few minutes of our attention to help him realize the fantasy that he was reveling in. We could have given him something that is increasingly hard to come by—a genuine sense of acceptance, appreciation, and belonging.

His fifteen minutes ended. Sporadic applause broke out from different parts of the gymnasium, echoing off the sterile white walls. The applause implied less an appreciation for his remarks than a collective gratitude for the conclusion of the speech. The audience was suddenly rejuvenated—the energy and mood had whipsawed noticeably.

We failed this man, and I was just as guilty as every other guest in the room. Why was it so hard to feign interest for fifteen minutes? What prevented us from making yet another donation that evening—one that would have had a far greater and more tangible impact on someone who was in more need than the tennis program at an affluent school?

* * *

Nobody cares. This has been one of the most alarming and fascinating components of entering adulthood. What we may have been used to while growing up—participation trophies, celebration for accomplishing even the most innate of tasks, a sense of impregnable egocentrism—it quickly reverses. Reality sets in—for the overwhelming majority of interactions, the harsh truth is that people just don't really care. Reciprocal appreciation only materializes if there is a direct impact on the recipient. If something is not relevant to the audience, then there is rarely any genuine attention or sense of regard.

This concept is nothing new or groundbreaking, but it does become increasingly apparent in adulthood. Those ribbons and awards disappear. You're no longer congratulated and celebrated for completing your homework. The invincibility inspired by being the center of attention at your preteen birthday party vanishes. The sharp contrast between the fallacy created during our childhoods and the reality confronted in adulthood is incredibly humbling.

And it can also be liberating. All of the time and energy we spend worrying about what everybody else is thinking of us, when, in reality, they probably aren't. They have their own lives, their own insecurities, their own day-to-day. What if we took all of that energy and angst, and reinvested it in ourselves and what we want to be—not what we worry others think we should be?

But that doesn't let us off the hook. Even if we shrug off other people's opinions, maybe we can still find it in ourselves to care. To have empathy, and to have heart. To take that late-night call from our friend, to show up for our grandparents' birthday, and to just be kind to someone, even if that means paying attention when the old guy babbles on for fifteen minutes.

THE MIRROR

My former roommate was furious. He had purchased a cheap wall mirror from a local discount store, and it had shattered as he was trying to hang it up. It was clearly a defective product, and on principle, he decided to take it back to the store to ask for an exchange. I had nothing to do at the time, so I decided to join him.

Once we arrived at the store, he immediately ambushed the cashier who had sold him the mirror a few hours prior. His tone was extremely inappropriate—he was belittling her. To him, it was as if she had singlehandedly created the defective product and then deliberately offloaded it on him. He was talking down to her (mind you, she was twice his age), and I was mortified. I remember trying to disappear in the back of the line—I wished that I could have become one of the lifeless items on the shelf behind them.

He was so blatantly disrespectful to this innocent woman. He was obviously angry because of what had happened, but he made no effort to approach the situation politely or rationally. He didn't treat the cashier as a person—he dehumanized her, and in the process, revealed so much about himself.

One of the greatest indicators of a person's character is how they handle situations like these and how they treat those who momentarily pass through their lives.

It is so easy to have respect for people that are in situations of power. Our bosses, successful acquaintances—anyone that we feel can be of help to us—we automatically treat these people well. I've seen that same roommate show deference and respect to an accomplished peer whom he had never met before. He was a different person, and I couldn't help but have flashbacks to the experience with him at the store only a few weeks prior. To him, there was something to be gained from this interaction. Whether it was furthering his career or being able to enter a new social group, this individual offered something to him. It was advantageous to treat him this way even though it was inauthentic—his demonstration of respect was entirely selfish.

But it's how we treat people who hold no sway over us that really matters. Every day, we encounter individuals whom we will never see again, who will bring us no financial gain, who offer no career advancement nor social stature. How we treat them truly defines who we are.

I look back at this mirror story now and I laugh at the irony. My former roommate was so furious about the cheap mirror that he had shattered, but he neglected to see what his actions were revealing. That mirror was trying to tell him something, and I think the reflection that it would have shown him every day would have been far more accurate than the replacement that currently hangs on his wall.

LIKE A ROLLING STONE

66 ou're going to become a rolling stone."

I had no idea what he was talking about. Was he referencing the rock band? He couldn't be as I had zero musical aspirations (and, more importantly, absolutely no singing talent). Was it a nod to the new life-style awaiting me in Los Angeles? That would be great, but knowing myself, very unlikely. Was he implying that I'd be wandering aimlessly for the next year? I hoped not—that was already a big insecurity of mine, and the last thing I needed was someone so dear to me telling me that I was making a mistake.

I eagerly awaited the explanation, and when it finally came, I couldn't help but smile—it's the perfect analogy for the mentality that I was trying to assume for my imminent move to Los Angeles.

My mentor told me that I needed to accumulate as many experiences as I possibly could. I had to open myself up to anything that may come across my path—confront it head-on and push forward. He said they may not all be enjoyable, positive, or even constructive at times, but they would still be important for my development nonetheless. He concluded that the collection of these experiences, no matter what they were, would eventually transform me into a rolling stone, picking up new pieces and particles along my path.

Norman Lear, a legendary television writer and producer, wrote a memoir entitled *Even This I Get to Experience*. This title is directly applicable to our early to mid-twenties. So much will happen to us during this phase in our lives, and we should open ourselves up to all of it with a conscious recognition that it is an opportunity for learning. Something that, no matter what it is, we, too, get to experience.

WITH GRATITUDE

Hi Team,

Today is my last day at the firm, and I want to take a moment to thank you for everything over the past three and a half years.

This firm has been a second home and an identity for me, and I'm filled with so much gratitude to have had the opportunity to work at such an extraordinary company. It truly has been a privilege to work with each of you.

My personal contact information is posted below, and I hope to stay in touch. Please don't hesitate to reach out to me if

you are ever in the Los Angeles area, and
I hope to see you again very soon.

With Gratitude,
Andrew Berman

O ver one hundred goodbyes. Hugs, handshakes, and personal contact information were exchanged.

I had grown up at this firm. It had been my fourth
official interview, my second internship, and my first real
foray into the professional world. It was so strange—I was
saying goodbye to a team that I genuinely admired, I was
leaving an office space that had come to resemble a second
home (complete with a fully stocked kitchen), and I was part-
ing with bosses and mentors that had far exceeded my expectations for what role models could be. More than the physical separation, I was also saying goodbye to the familiar—a
set routine, responsibilities and assignments for which I had
become self-sufficient, and a leadership position that had
forced me to grow far more than I had originally anticipated.

I'll never forget my last exit from the building. I cleaned
up my desk, turned in my access card, and walked outside
carrying nothing more than a briefcase filled with leftover
items that I had accumulated over the years. A few errant
pieces of scratch paper, licensing certificates, notebooks,
pens, and business cards. Everything was so trivial, but I felt

possessed to take them with me. I didn't want to say goodbye; every piece of that desk was a connection back to the monumental chapter in my life that was coming to an end.

Once I finally managed to drag myself out of the building, I took a brief moment to pause and reflect on the significance of the occasion. Leaving this firm was much more than a job switch to me—it was a loss of identity. My entire post-college life had revolved around it. The late nights and early mornings as the youngest analyst on the team, desperate to prove myself and start my career off on the right foot. The various licensing exams and all of the hours spent memorizing financial regulatory rules. The opportunity to help lead an incredible team of nine analysts after two and a half years of paying dues, and all of the invaluable lessons that they unexpectedly taught me. The close friends and relationships that I had been lucky enough to cultivate in a city that never felt like home.

In the weeks leading up to my departure, I think I changed my mind about leaving at least five times. There were several mini panic attacks, countless numbers of distressed phone calls to friends and family, and even a meeting with my boss to discuss whether or not I could undo the exit process that had already been started.

I repeatedly asked myself—why was I leaving? It was an amazing job. A smart, ethical, and progressive firm that was growing rapidly. My role had significant potential. I was letting go of this—a reliable and set path—for a complete unknown.

As the loss of identity started to resonate, I became terrified. When people asked me where I worked (an unfortunately overused icebreaker), what would I say? I'm joining a start-up? I'm a writer? (Talk about a dramatic departure from a reliable finance job.) I'm in a transitional period? All of these were my truths, but I didn't like them.

I hadn't officially left yet, but I was already nostalgic for the life that I had spent the past three and half years building in New York. My title, my team, my known career path, my friends, my set routine—everything was vanishing. I was taking a leap of faith into yet another unknown—would I undo all of the progress that I had tirelessly worked for since graduation? Was I restarting? What about the massive pay cut that I was about to take? What if I wanted to go back—would the firm have me? What about the social life that I had built for myself in New York? What if I came to find myself alone in an old city that wasn't how I remembered it, without the safety net of an amazing job and close college friends?

As the panic subsided, I found peace in an emotion that I never thought I'd feel at such a stressful time: gratitude. I was grateful for everything that I had been able to learn and experience over the past three and a half years. All of the challenges, setbacks, and successes at work. The failed long-distance relationship—all of the great times and the lessons that I learned from the painful ones. The string of inconsistent and eccentric dating experiences from my single life in New York. The lifelong friends that I had made and all of the incredible nights that we spent together. The promotion to a management role at a great firm with a collection of such talented people.

I found peace in the realization that I was walking out of the office that evening with far more than the small bag of disorganized items—I was leaving with a collection of so many amazing experiences that I had been lucky enough to have. These experiences, all of which I continue to carry with me today, have formed my backbone—a confidence that reminds me that I'll be able to handle anything that is thrown my way. A feeling that reassures me that no matter how intimidating, challenging, or disappointing the unknown path in front of me may become at times, it represents another experience that I get to live through.

EPILOGUE:
CALIFORNICATION

The home is eerily lively and jubilant. Laughter reverberates down the long entryway, echoing off the newly repainted and unblemished walls. Light pours in from each of the many uncovered windows, staging the scene with a gentle brightness that is both becoming and welcoming.

Each room assumes a life of its own. The newly furnished living room is a preview for the gatherings that lie ahead—reunions with old friends, late nights with significant others, and evenings with new acquaintances. The kitchen, with its recently cleaned and bare countertops, teases at the surprisingly adequate meals that will be painstakingly prepared amidst a mess of pots and pans. Most notably, my room is open and vacant—brimming with potential for its new occupant and a completely new way life.

I find myself filled with joy and excitement. There is no yearning or nostalgia for memories of times that have long since passed. There is so much opportunity on the horizon that I can't help but revel in my own cautious optimism. A new city, a new job, and a new state of mind—it is eagerly ushered in and greeted with an open embrace.

I am moving to Los Angeles for nobody other than myself. I have given three and a half years to New York City, each defined by its own series of challenging and magical experiences. It is time for a change because *I* feel that it is time. I have been pulled by an ex-girlfriend, pressured by friends and family members, pushed by repetition at a first job, and tempted by the longing for my hometown and its soothing familiarity. These factors, however charged they may have been in their time, hold no power over me today. I make the decision to come home as my own independent adult—assuming full responsibility and ownership over my departure from one set path and my entrance onto yet another unknown.

*　*　*

How do you end something that never felt like it officially began? Twenty-six months of writing and reflecting, and I still feel that I've barely begun to scratch the surface of what needs to be done. I now acknowledge that there will never be definitive closure. The memories of my experiences in New York City and the lessons that they've taught me are scattered through every page of this text, but they will never be perfectly finalized. They are today and forever will be amorphous, evolving with the new perspective that I gain as I continue my journey into adulthood.

I've also come to accept the fact that I haven't grown up, and that's okay. I'm not sure if anybody ever really does. I still find myself drifting between so many different states—flashes of confidence where I feel that I am doing exactly what I am meant to do, blips of excitement where I'm inspired by the optionality and opportunity that lay ahead, periods of angst and worry that I still haven't found my permanent passion, moments of sadness that I still haven't found my life partner, and times of joy where I revel in the fact that I'm fully engaged and present in my surroundings.

As I write the very last paragraphs of this work, I realize that the title is completely misleading. The irony is both humbling and pacifying. The boy who stepped down from that graduation stage nearly four years ago with a diploma and a ticket into the real world hasn't fully grown up. In many ways, he is still just as wide-eyed, confused, and excitable today as he was on that very sunny morning in a partially filled football stadium surrounded by thousands of his peers. And I wish to celebrate this. I want to revel in the fact that he hasn't lost the sense of intrigue, passion, vulnerability, and curiosity that he held so dearly back then. I hope that he never does, because only then will he have proven this title to be true.

The text comes to an end, but in many ways, it is just beginning. These pages will continue to be filled for many years to come, lined with the experiences of everything that I'm fortunate enough to encounter on this surprisingly magnificent journey.

Then We Grew Up. Not quite yet.

MEET THE AUTHOR

Andrew Berman graduated from the University of Pennsylvania in 2014. He was previously an Associate at an asset management firm based in Greenwich, Connecticut. He currently lives in Los Angeles, California, and is working at a healthcare startup. Like so many others, he is still trying to navigate his twenties.